FOLD ME UP

Dear Janice,

this life, this wonderful
life, is on your side.

This universe, this wonderful
universe is in your corner. Trust
that and let it give you strength
when the future seems uncertain.
Love Always, Regina

FOLD ME UP

----

100 Paper Fortune-Tellers
for Life's Pressing Questions

Michelle Taute

Designs by Kelly N. Kofron

A PERIGEE BOOK

A PERIGEE BOOK
Published by the Penguin Group
Penguin Group (USA) LLC
375 Hudson Street, New York, New York 10014

USA | Canada | UK | Ireland | Australia | New Zealand | India | South Africa | China

penguin.com

A Penguin Random House Company

FOLD ME UP

ISBN: 978-0-399-16330-2

First edition: November 2013

PRINTED IN THE UNITED STATES OF AMERICA

10   9   8   7   6   5   4   3   2   1

Designs by Kelly N. Kofron

While the author has made every effort to provide accurate telephone numbers, Internet
addresses, and other contact information at the time of publication, neither the publisher nor
the author assumes any responsibility for errors, or for changes that occur after publication.
Further, the publisher does not have any control over and does not assume any
responsibility for author or third-party websites or their content.

Most Perigee books are available at special quantity discounts for bulk purchases for sales
promotions, premiums, fund-raising, or educational use. Special books, or book excerpts, can also
be created to fit specific needs. For details, write: Special.Markets@us.penguingroup.com.

Paper Fortune-Tellers Tell All

(Or, Cootie Catchers Aren't Just for Kids)

There's something pretty magical about this book. I mean mind-blowing, reality-defying, I-can't-believe-my-eyes kind of magical. The 100 cootie catchers that follow transform ordinary sheets of paper into powerful, awe-inspiring devices—ones that can predict the future, spit out words of encouragement, help you apologize in style, or just dish out bits of wisdom.

What's that? You don't know what the heck a cootie catcher is? Oh, sure you do. Just forget your age for a few seconds. We're going to take a little trip back in time. Way back to the third or fourth grade. That's when it typically hits: the cootie catcher craze. We're talking about those little paper fortune-tellers you and your classmates fashioned out of notebook paper.

Except now these childhood toys can answer adult problems. Need help with a major life decision? Just consult the "100% accurate answers to any yes or no question" cootie catcher. Forget a birthday? Get out of hot water with a cootie catcher that doubles as a gift and greeting card. Wondering where the heck your soul mate is? There's a cootie catcher that knows. Hate Jordan almonds? How about an awesome cootie catcher as your wedding favor?

With 100 cootie catchers, *Fold Me Up* has every age, occasion, and pressing life question covered. And they're all tricked out with swank design and/or illustration. After all, this isn't kid stuff. It's serious, adult cootie catcher business.

Happy paper fortune-telling!

—Michelle Taute

P.S. What? You need more than 100 cootie catchers? Find more paper fortune-teller goodness at paperfortunetellers.com.

TOP SECRET COOTIE CATCHER
ASSEMBLY INSTRUCTIONS*

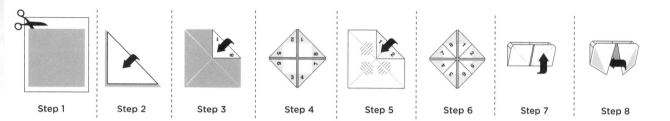

| Step 1 | Step 2 | Step 3 | Step 4 | Step 5 | Step 6 | Step 7 | Step 8 |

Step 1: Choose a cootie catcher. Then cut around the edges of the square to remove it from this book. (Yes, it's OK to cut a book in this particular instance. Just don't run with the scissors.)

Step 2: Pick up one corner of the square and fold it across to the opposite corner. Unfold and repeat by folding the opposite two corners together. Unfold again. The fold creases should form an "X" that marks the middle of your cootie catcher to help guide folding.

Step 3: With the text side facing down, fold up all four corners of the cootie catcher to the center. (Failure to do so may interfere with this device's fortune-telling abilities.)

Step 4: Does it look like this? If not, go back to Step 1 and start over.

Step 5: Flip the paper over and fold up all four corners again.

---

* Cootie catchers are known to have almost magical abilities to predict the future. But we must advise you NOT to base any major life decisions—or heck, your dinner order—solely on the advice of this device. The lawyers we couldn't afford made us say this.

Step 6: Does your Cootie Catcher look like this? No? Go back to Step 1 and start over.

Step 7: Fold in half as shown. Remind yourself that this process is, indeed, top secret.

Step 8: Place your fingers under the four paper flaps to pop the device up. Then work the cootie catcher back and forth to form creases. Commence amusing friends and enemies with your new fortune-telling abilities. (See "How to Play" on the next page.)

HOW TO PLAY

Thinking all the way back to grade school can make your brain hurt. So here's a little refresher—a cheat sheet if you will—on how to use all these great paper fortune-tellers.

Step 1: Pick one of the words, numbers, or letters on the top of the cootie catcher. Work the cootie catcher back and forth as you count up to the number (1, 2, 3, 4), spell out the letters in the word (c-o-o-t-i-e), or say the alphabet up to the letter (A, B, C, D, E). If you picked 2, for instance, you'd move it back and forth only two times. No words or numbers? Spell out the most prevalent color in the illustration or spell out what the illustration depicts (e.g., pig).

Step 2: Now pick one of the words, numbers, or letters on view inside the paper fortune-teller. Then work the cootie catcher back and forth again as you count up to the number (1, 2, 3, 4) or spell out the word (c-o-o-t-i-e).

Step 3: OK, it's time to make a final selection. Pick one of the letters or numbers on view inside the cootie catcher. Then lift up the flap and reveal the message! Some cootie catchers predict the future. Others answer a pressing question or give a fortune on a specific topic.

Step 4: Repeat as needed. You can rock a paper fortune-teller alone or with a friend. They even make popular party guests.

100% ACCURATE ANSWERS* TO ANY YES OR NO QUESTION

This piece of paper can predict the future, make tough decisions, and generally boss you around.

Hard to say—
getting mixed psychic
signals right now.

No.
Now stop asking
so many questions
already.

Better flip a coin.
Heads means yes.
Tails means no.

Yep—
feeling a definite
yes vibe.

Yes.
A thousand
times yes.

No.
Did you really just
ask that question?

Nope. Negative.
No way.

Affirmative.
Absolutely. Yes!

WILL I EVER BE RICH OR FAMOUS?

Sure, you have mad skills and big dreams. But only this cootie catcher knows if they'll pay off.

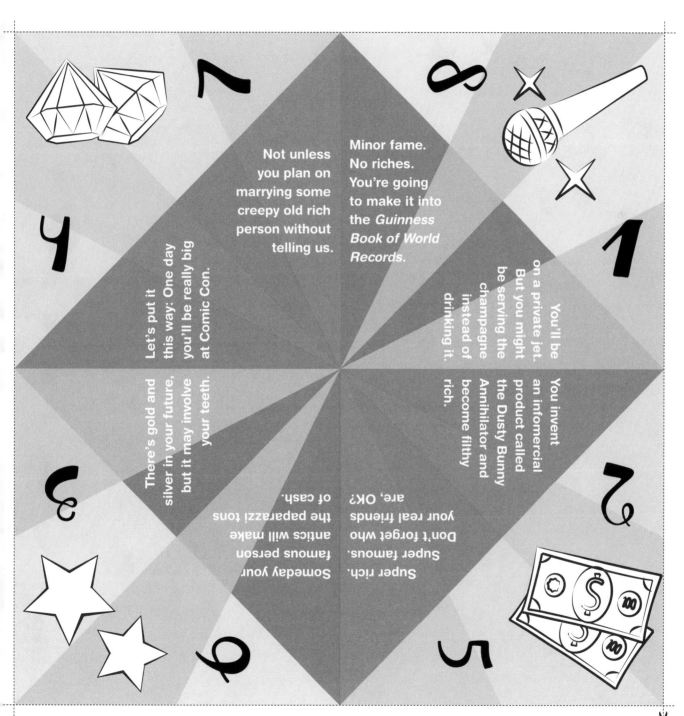

I'M BREAKING UP WITH YOU (WITH THIS COOTIE CATCHER)

Dumping people via text is so over. Let this fortune-teller do the dirty work for you.

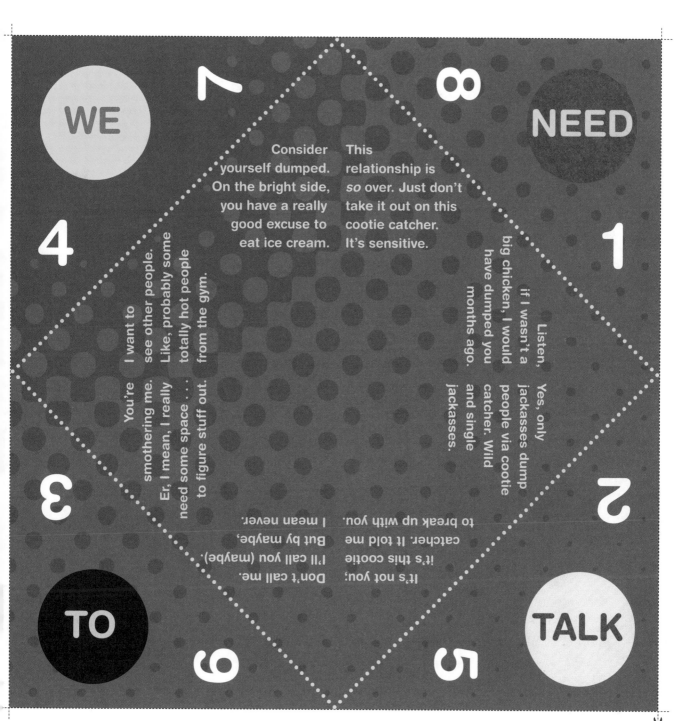

WILL A SHARK ATTACK?

Practice safe swimming. Don't go in the water without consulting this cootie catcher.

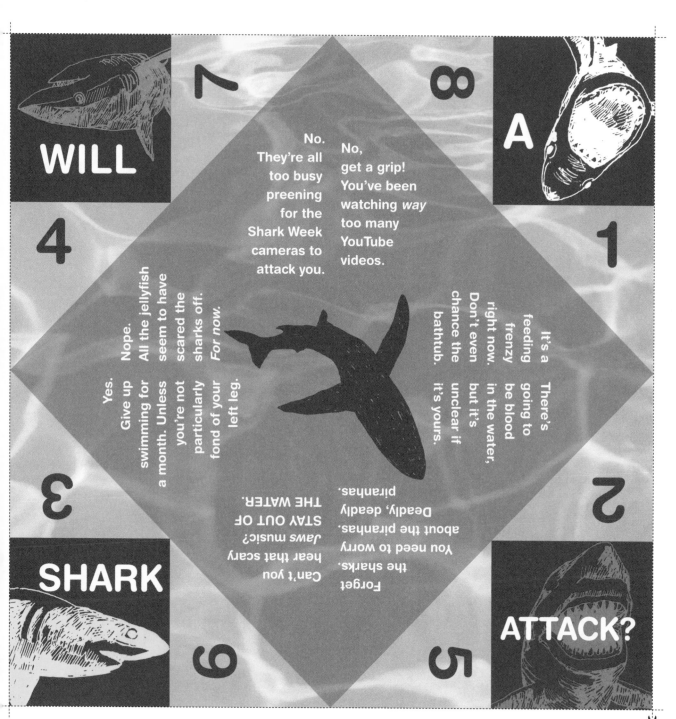

WILL

A

SHARK

ATTACK?

7

8

4

1

3

2

6

5

No. They're all too busy preening for the Shark Week cameras to attack you.

No, get a grip! You've been watching *way* too many YouTube videos.

Nope. All the jellyfish seem to have scared the sharks off. *For now.*

It's a feeding frenzy right now. There's going to be blood in the water, Don't even chance the bathtub. but it's unclear if it's yours.

Yes. Give up swimming for a month. Unless you're not particularly fond of your left leg.

Can't you hear that scary *Jaws* music? STAY OUT OF THE WATER.

Forget the sharks. You need to worry about the piranhas. Deadly, deadly piranhas.

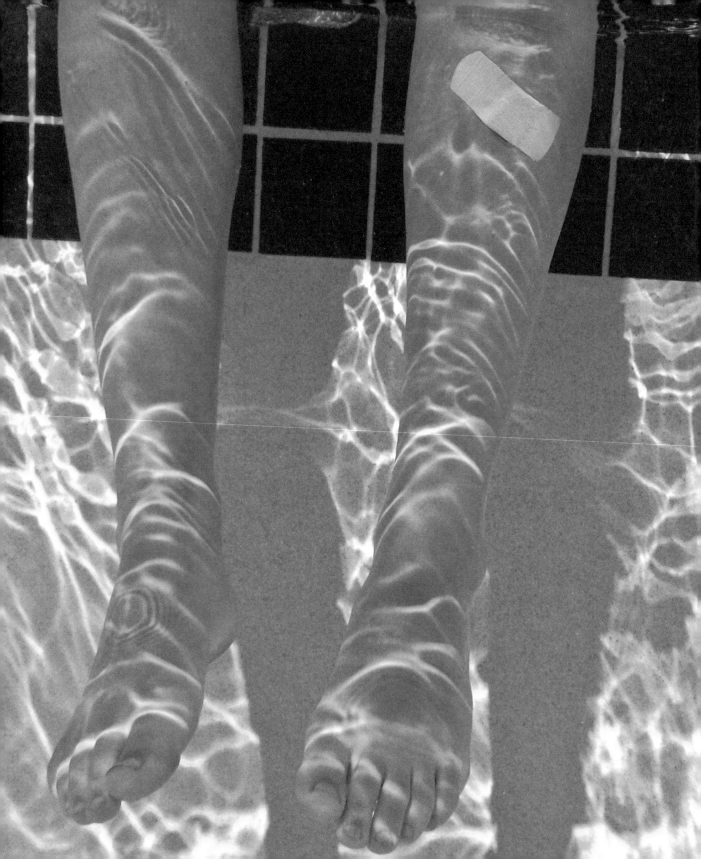

WILL I LIVE WITH MY PARENTS FOREVER?

Whoa, you're an adult living at home. Let's find out when this situation might end.

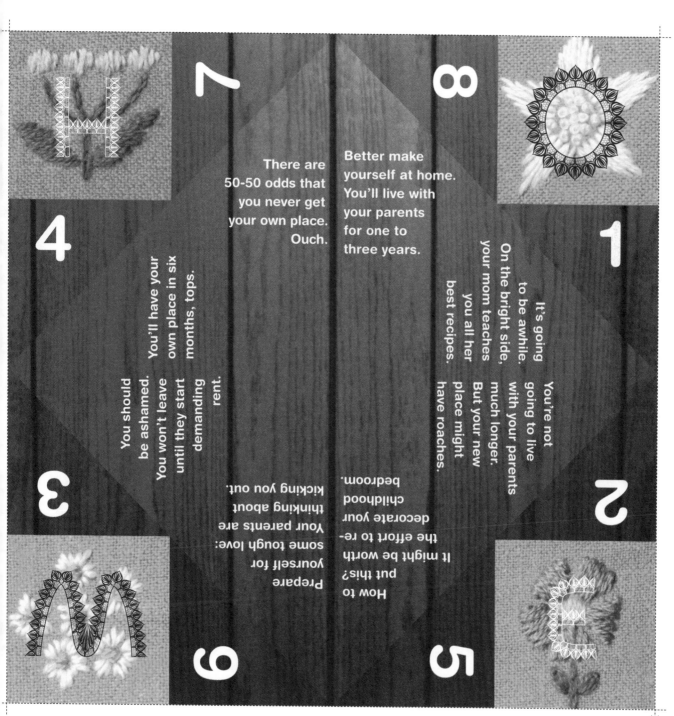

7

There are 50-50 odds that you never get your own place. Ouch.

8

Better make yourself at home. You'll live with your parents for one to three years.

4

You'll have your own place in six months, tops.

1

It's going to be awhile. You're not going to live with your parents much longer. On the bright side, your mom teaches you all her best recipes. But your new place might have roaches.

3

You should be ashamed. You won't leave until they start demanding rent.

Prepare yourself for some tough love: Your parents are thinking about kicking you out.

How to put this? It might be worth the effort to re-decorate your childhood bedroom.

2

9

5

WILL MY CREDIT CARD GET DECLINED?

Avoid embarrassment and dirty looks with this handy-dandy cootie catcher.

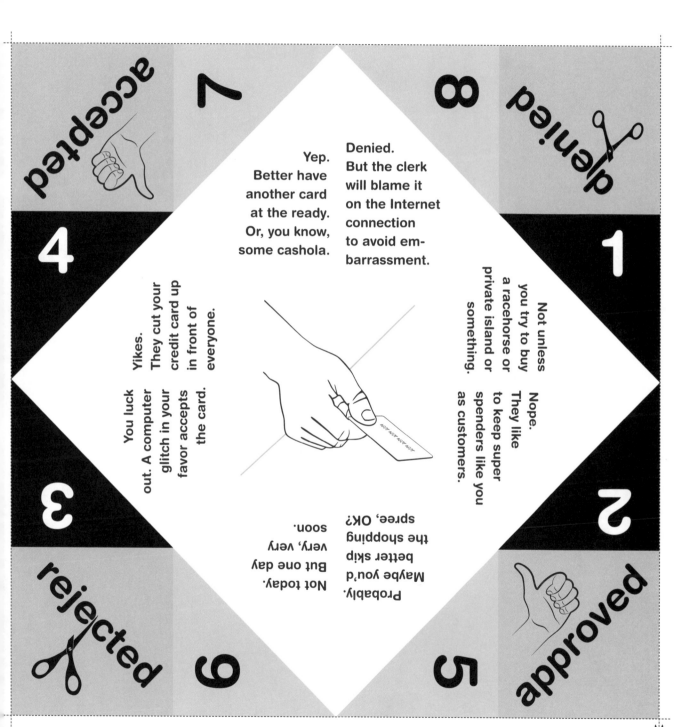

AM I A GOOD KISSER?

You need to know the truth. Do you make them go weak in the knees or run for the hills?

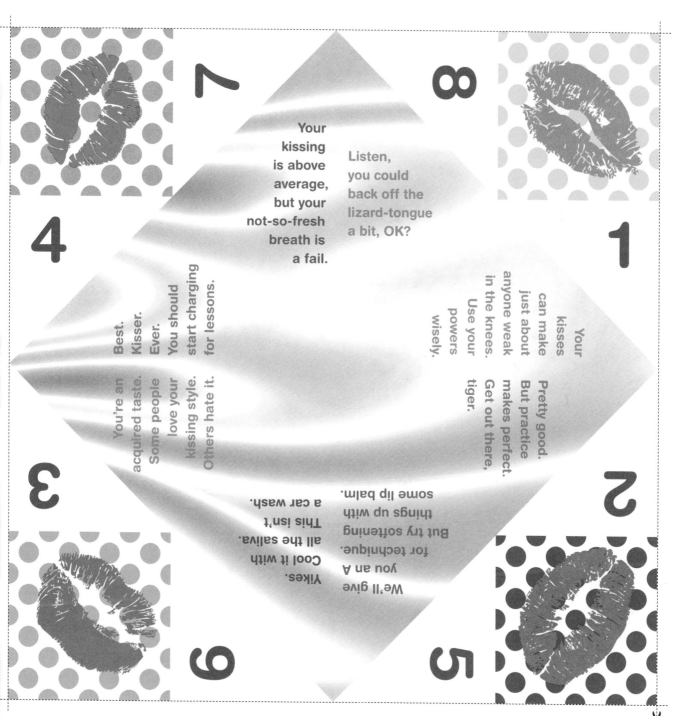

7

8

Your kissing is above average, but your not-so-fresh breath is a fail.

Listen, you could back off the lizard-tongue a bit, OK?

4

1

Best. Kisser. Ever. You should start charging for lessons.

You're an acquired taste. Some people love your kissing style. Others hate it.

Your kisses can make just about anyone weak in the knees. Use your powers wisely.

Pretty good. But practice makes perfect. Get out there, tiger.

3

2

Yikes. Cool it with all the saliva. This isn't a car wash.

We'll give you an A for technique. But try softening things up with some lip balm.

9

5

AM I HIGH MAINTENANCE?

Don't put it off anymore. Find out if you suffer from this silent friendship killer.

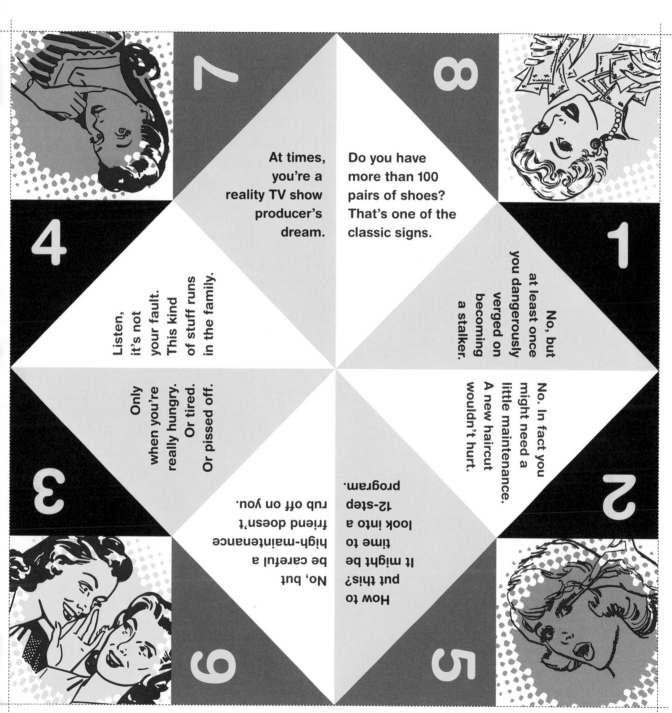

At times, you're a reality TV show producer's dream.

Do you have more than 100 pairs of shoes? That's one of the classic signs.

No, but at least once you dangerously verged on becoming a stalker. A new haircut wouldn't hurt.

No. In fact you might need a little maintenance.

Listen, it's not your fault. This kind of stuff runs in the family.

Only when you're really hungry. Or tired. Or pissed off.

No, but be careful a high-maintenance friend doesn't rub off on you.

How to put this? It might be time to look into a 12-step program.

EMERGENCY SELF-CONFIDENCE BOOSTER

Illustrated by Jessica Jones

Looks like a pretty desk accessory. Secretly spits out words of encouragement on demand.

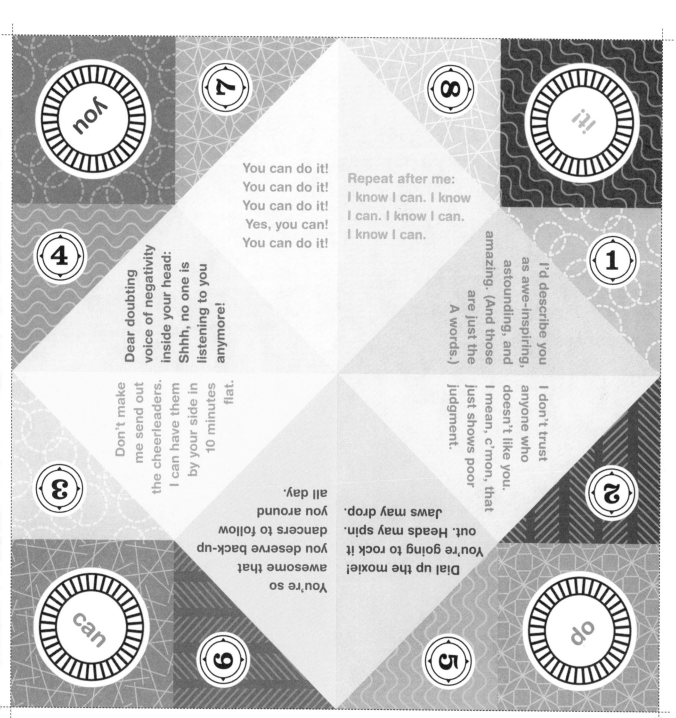

I FORGOT YOUR BIRTHDAY, BUT HERE'S A COOTIE CATCHER

Sometimes, you're a crappy friend. Redeem yourself with this awesome birthday fortune-teller.

I

7

8

forgot

4

1

Umm, fortune-tellers are worth, like, 10 cards. This is a supercharged birthday wish.

Hop in my time machine. We'll go back to your birthday for more cake and ice cream.

Umm, I'm a dis-organized procrastinator. But I made you this birthday cootie catcher!

Can I call a do-over? Let's pretend this showed up exactly on your birthday.

One day isn't enough to celebrate your awesomeness. I timed this to stretch out the festivities.

Look at it this way. Now you get to have a birthday month. Way better than one day.

3

2

your

6

5

birth day

Did I say happy birthday, yet? Happy, happy birthday!

Hey, stale birthday wishes are way better than stale cake. Also, you're the best!

INSTANT LIE DETECTOR TEST

Forget the FBI. Just say a statement then test its veracity with this magical cootie catcher.

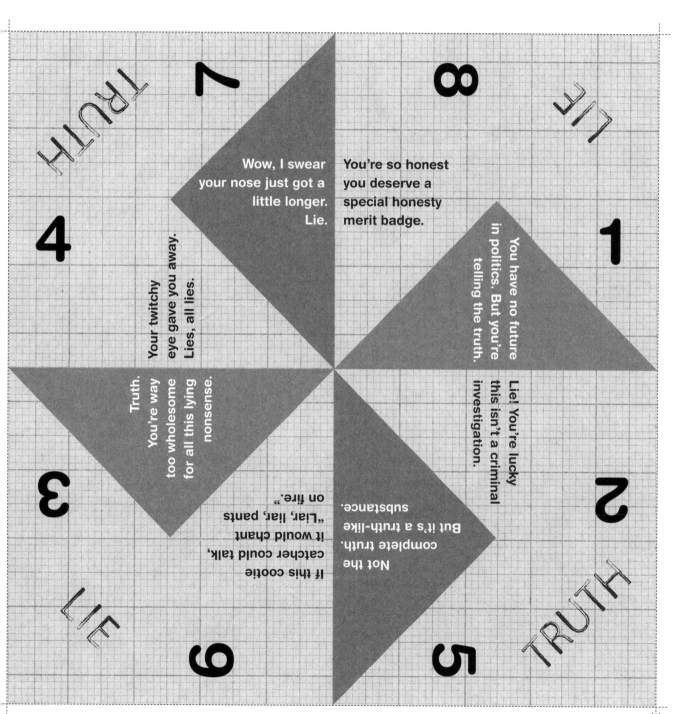

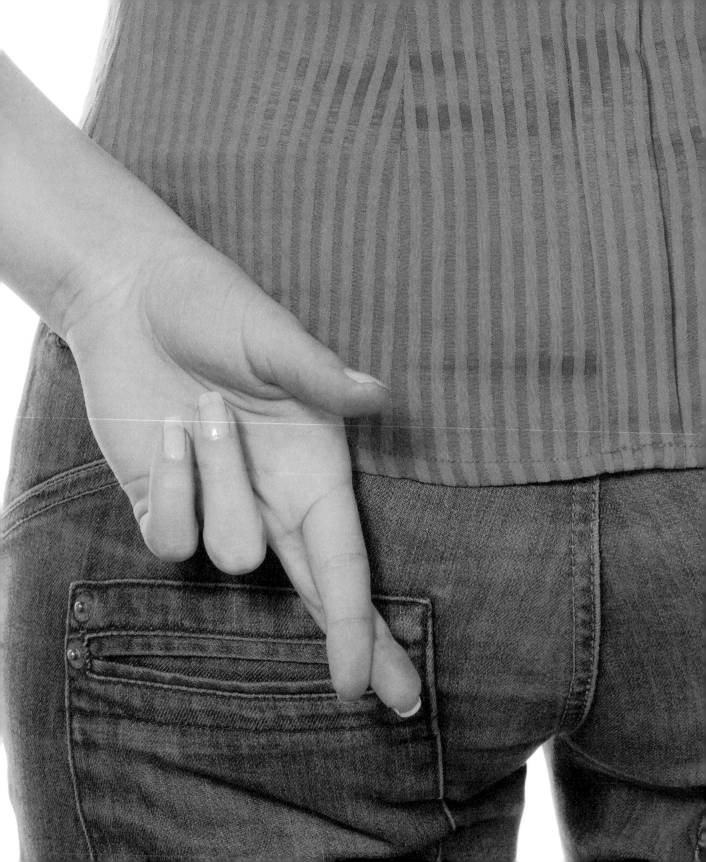

MY '80S MOVIE ALTER EGO

Ladies, you were meant to be '80s movie stars (obviously). Now find out which one.

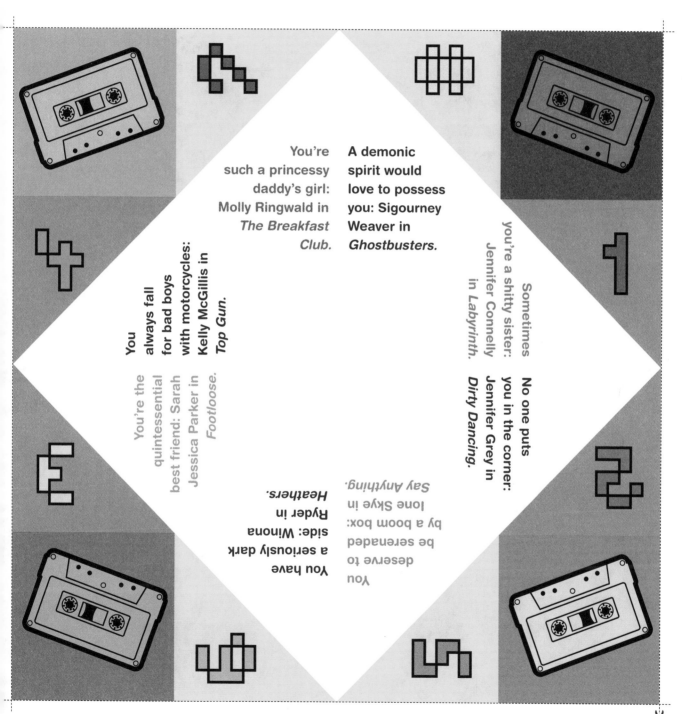

You're such a princessy daddy's girl: Molly Ringwald in *The Breakfast Club.*

A demonic spirit would love to possess you: Sigourney Weaver in *Ghostbusters.*

Sometimes you're a shitty sister: Jennifer Connelly in *Labyrinth.*

You always fall for bad boys with motorcycles: Kelly McGillis in *Top Gun.*

No one puts you in the corner: Jennifer Grey in *Dirty Dancing.*

You're the quintessential best friend: Sarah Jessica Parker in *Footloose.*

You have a seriously dark side: Winona Ryder in *Heathers.*

You deserve to be serenaded by a boom box: Ione Skye in *Say Anything.*

I REALLY, REALLY HATE YOU

The perfect passive-aggressive gift for any enemy. Fold it up and leave in said enemy's path.

7

When you come within five feet of me, it takes all my willpower not to stick out my tongue.

8

I find you more unpleasant than wearing the same underwear seven days in a row.

REALLY

4

You're lucky I don't believe in voodoo dolls or curses or public shaming.

1

My hatred for you is so powerful that it's slowly eating away the lining of my stomach.

It's more of a grudge, really, than all-out hatred. But, hey, you know what you did.

3

I hate you more than mushy peas. And dirty public restrooms. And food poisoning.

You're pretty much my arch enemy. So don't be asking to borrow a cup of sugar or anything.

Being near you makes me break out in hives and start scratching almost un-controllably.

2

HATE

9

5

YOU

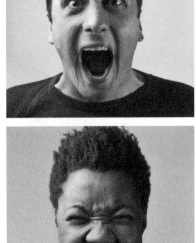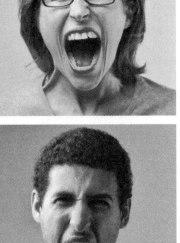

I REALLY, REALLY LOVE YOU

Illustrated by Lisa Congdon

The depth of your love is impressive. Give this to the object of your affection posthaste.

7 · I

8 · you

4

1

I love you more than Pizza Rolls. And hula hoops. And funny Internet videos.

If I wasn't such a nature-loving hippie, I'd carve our initials into a tree with a heart around them.

You make me go weak in the knees. And sometimes, strangely, the elbows, too.

Love is a four-letter word, but I'm still willing to shout out my feelings for you in public places.

Looking at you makes me feel all sweet and mushy inside— kinda like a pudding-filled cupcake.

It wasn't love at first sight exactly. Probably third sight. And every time thereafter.

3

2

I mean, what says true love and romance more than a cootie catcher?

I love you so much I don't even mind it when you fall asleep on my shoulder and drool a little.

really

9

5

love

DO I HAVE BEDBUGS?

Oh, ick. We're sorry you even feel the need to cut this one out and fold it up.

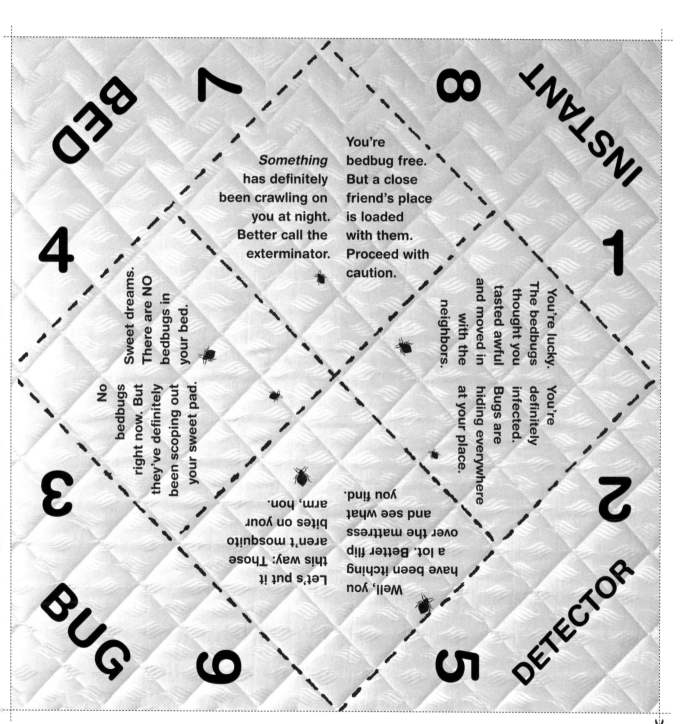

INSTANT BED BUG DETECTOR

1. You're lucky. You're bedbug free. But a close friend's place is loaded with them. Proceed with caution.

2. Well, you have been itching a lot. Better flip over the mattress and see what you find.

3. No bedbugs right now. But they've definitely been scoping out your sweet pad.

4. Sweet dreams. There are NO bedbugs in your bed.

5. The bedbugs definitely thought you tasted awful and moved in with the neighbors.

6. Let's put it this way: Those aren't mosquito bites on your arm, hon.

7. *Something* has definitely been crawling on you at night. Better call the exterminator.

8. You're bedbug free. But a close friend's place is loaded with them. Proceed with caution.

You're lucky. The bedbugs definitely thought you tasted awful and moved in with the neighbors. Bugs are hiding everywhere at your place.

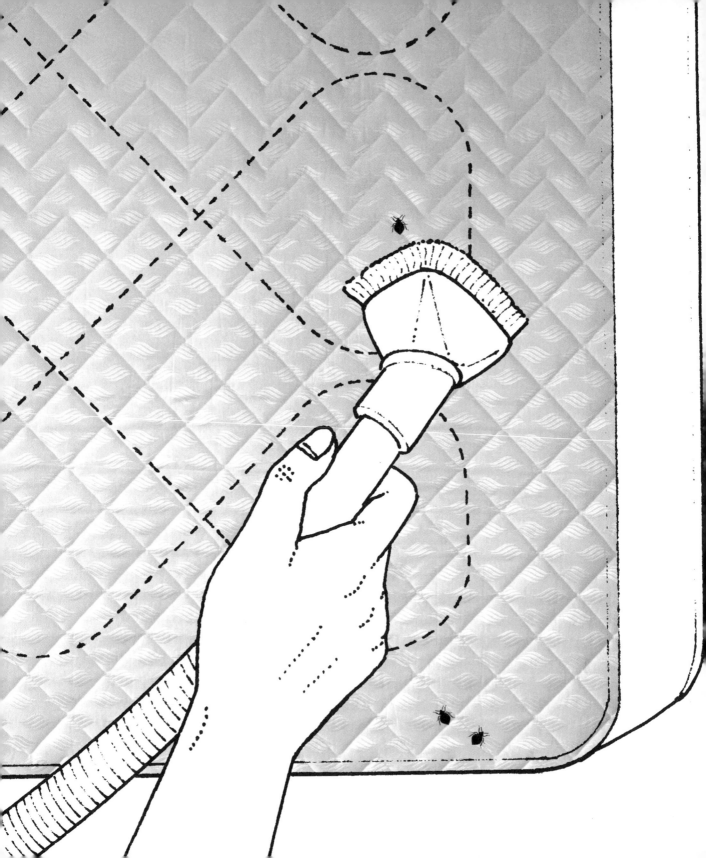

DOES MY BOSS SECRETLY HATE ME?

Yikes. This is a tricky situation. Better get some career expertise from this fortune-teller.

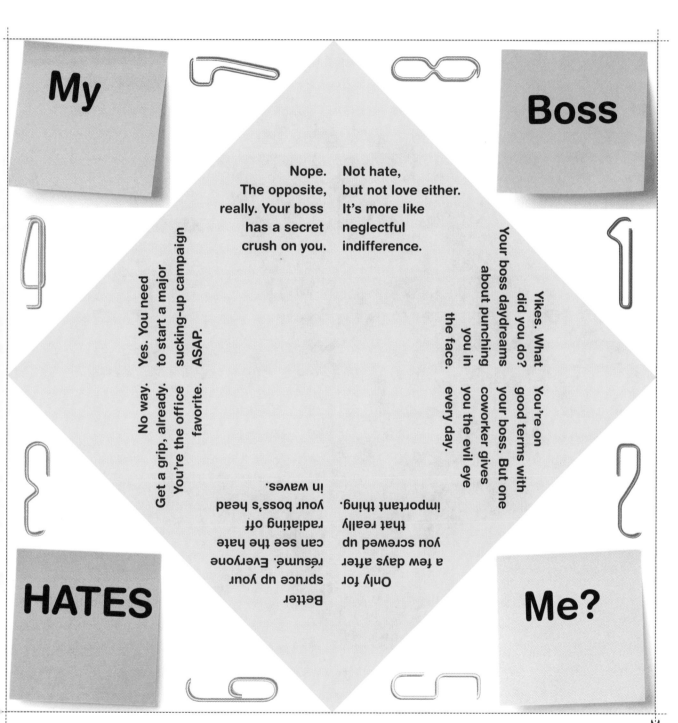

My

Boss

HATES

Me?

Nope. The opposite, really. Your boss has a secret crush on you.

Not hate, but not love either. It's more like neglectful indifference.

Your boss daydreams about punching you in the face. every day.

Yikes. What did you do? You're on good terms with your boss. But one coworker gives you the evil eye

Yes. You need to start a major sucking-up campaign ASAP.

No way. Get a grip, already. You're the office favorite.

Better spruce up your résumé. Everyone can see the hate radiating off your boss's head in waves.

Only for a few days after you screwed up that really important thing.

MAKE YOUR OWN: BEST FRIENDS FOREVER

You're never too old for a BFF. Fill in the fortunes with the reasons your best friend rocks.

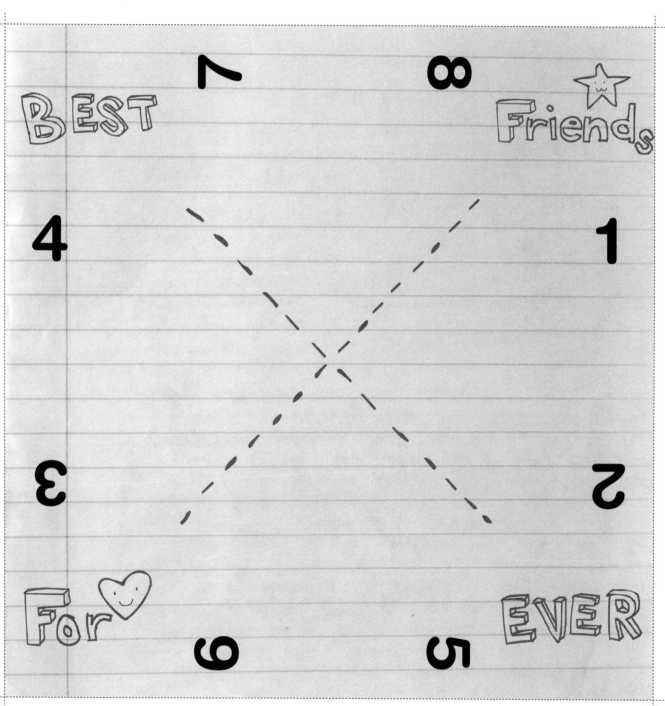

DOES MY CRUSH LIKE ME BACK?

Putting yourself out there is brave. But wusses will want to consult this cootie catcher first.

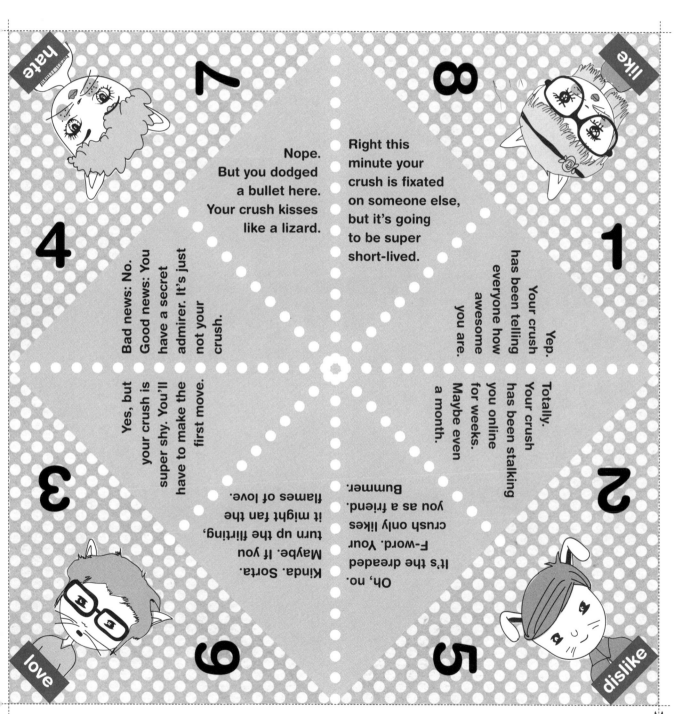

hate

like

7

8

4

1

Nope. But you dodged a bullet here. Your crush kisses like a lizard.

Right this minute your crush is fixated on someone else, but it's going to be super short-lived.

Bad news: No. Good news: You have a secret admirer. It's just not your crush.

Yep. Totally. Your crush has been telling everyone how awesome you are. Your crush has been stalking you online for weeks. Maybe even a month.

Yes, but your crush is super shy. You'll have to make the first move.

Kinda. Sorta. Maybe. If you turn up the flirting, it might fan the flames of love.

Oh, no. It's the dreaded F-word. Your crush only likes you as a friend. Bummer.

3

2

love

dislike

9

5

MY JANE AUSTEN CHARACTER

OK, book geek. Here's who you'd really be in one of Miss Austen's famous novels.

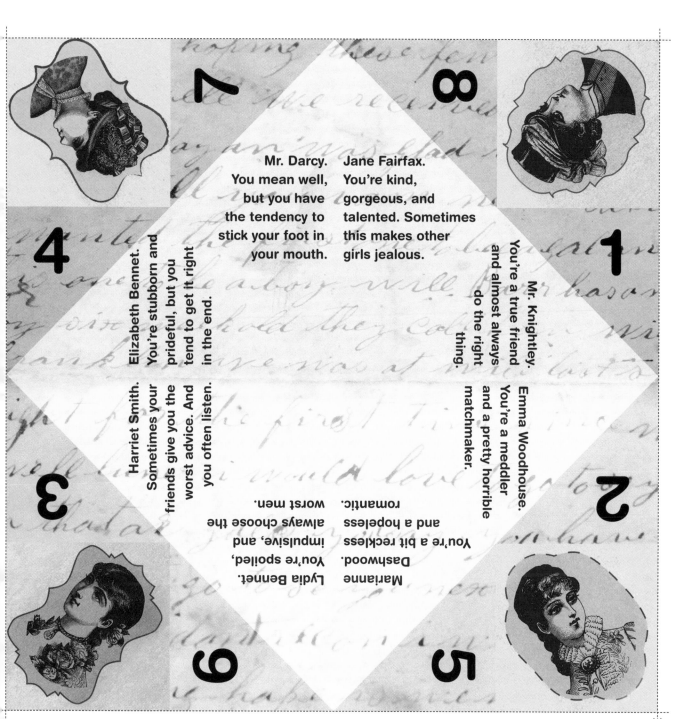

7

8

4

1

Mr. Darcy. You mean well, but you have the tendency to stick your foot in your mouth.

Jane Fairfax. You're kind, gorgeous, and talented. Sometimes this makes other girls jealous.

Mr. Knightley. You're a true friend and almost always do the right thing.

Emma Woodhouse. You're a meddler and a pretty horrible matchmaker.

Elizabeth Bennet. You're stubborn and prideful, but you tend to get it right in the end.

Harriet Smith. Sometimes your friends give you the worst advice. And you often listen.

3

Lydia Bennet. You're spoiled, impulsive, and always choose the worst men.

Marianne Dashwood. You're a bit reckless and a hopeless romantic.

2

6

5

time hoping these few lines
all well we received you
friday an was glad to hea
i tell you i am never
anted the first one to bee a ga
one to be a boy will Barr ho
six week old they call hi
nklin we was at will loo
t for the first time sin
ll luner i would love to go to
that ar gald you say you ha
art to go to se you nex sat
but dad recon i will ge

WHY IS THE SKY BLUE?

A big philosophical question for a humble little cootie catcher. Let's do this!

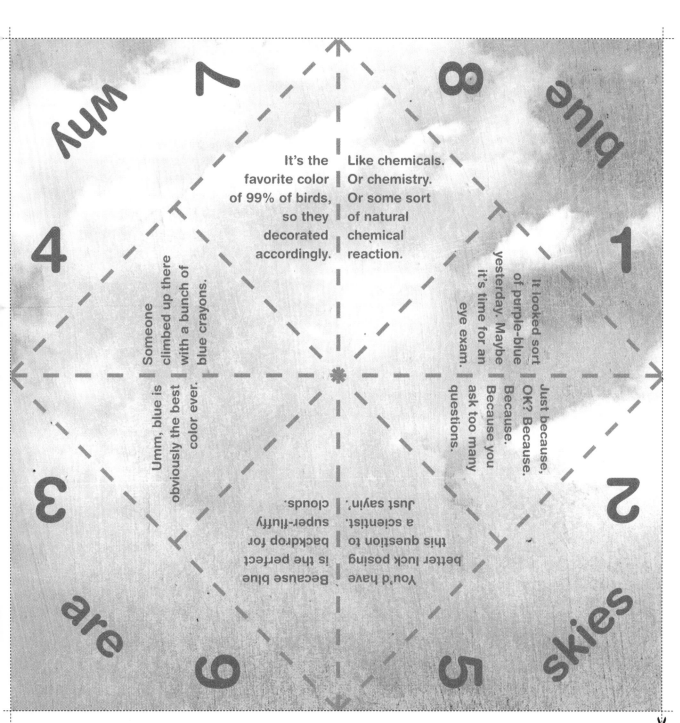

CALORIE-FREE EMERGENCY CUPCAKES

OK, you can't eat them. But the fortunes inside will still give you (or a friend) a sugar buzz.

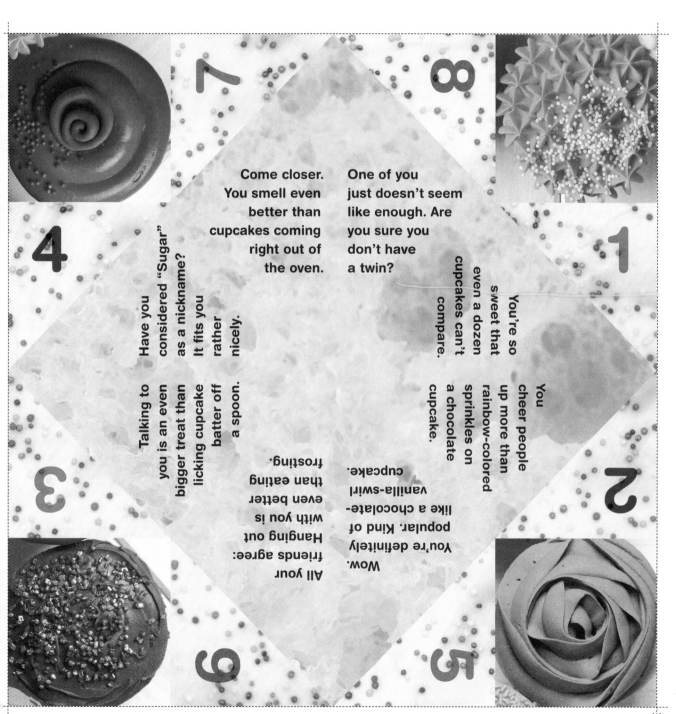

7

8

4

1

Come closer. You smell even better than cupcakes coming right out of the oven.

One of you just doesn't seem like enough. Are you sure you don't have a twin?

Have you considered "Sugar" as a nickname? It fits you rather nicely.

You're so sweet that even a dozen cupcakes can't compare.

You cheer people up more than rainbow-colored sprinkles on a chocolate cupcake.

Talking to you is an even bigger treat than licking cupcake batter off a spoon.

All your friends agree: Hanging out with you is even better than eating frosting.

Wow. You're definitely popular. Kind of like a chocolate-vanilla-swirl cupcake.

3

6

2

5

AM I IN LOVE?

I mean, it feels like you're in love. But is it really true? Or are you stuck in a hormone haze?

ARE 7

8 **LOVE?**

4

1

Kinda. Sorta. Maybe. It's too early to make a real call. Give things a little time to develop.

You're totally crazily in love. Try to keep the PDA to a minimum. Some of us are single.

It's only lust, hon. Enjoy it while it lasts, but don't expect happily ever after or anything.

is definitely some strong friendship and affection.

It's not love, per se. But there

You're definitely in love. A bunch of invisible cupids are flying around your head right now.

No. You're just indulging in some wishful thinking. Hold out for the real thing.

3

2

YOU

IN

9

5

It's love with a capital L. Back away, please. No one wants to witness any mushiness.

Not yet. But it might happen. These things can take a little time to blossom.

I

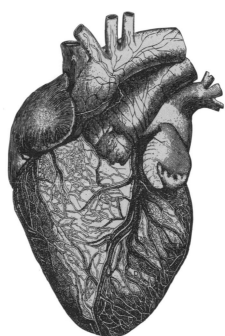

YOU

WILL MY CAT VIDEO GO VIRAL?

Your cat is cute, for sure. But will you cash in with millions of Internet views? Find out now.

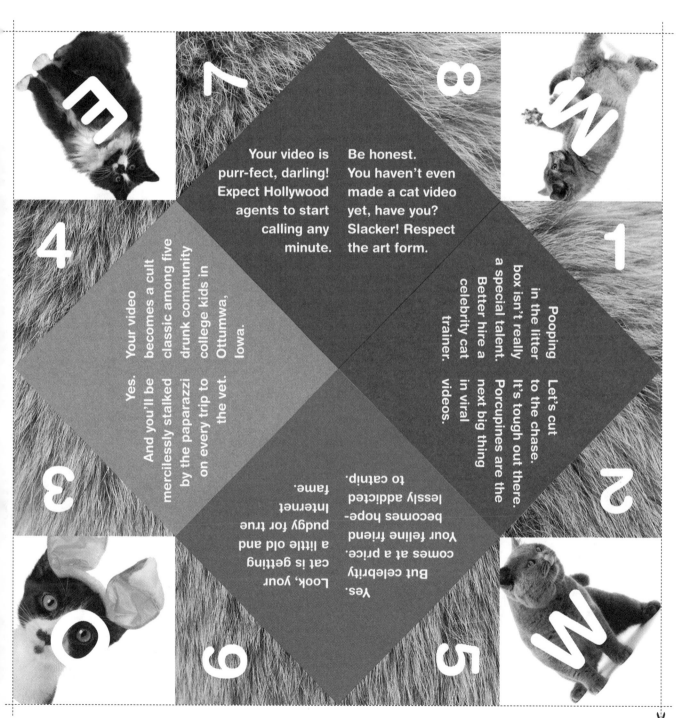

7

Your video is purr-fect, darling! Expect Hollywood agents to start calling any minute.

8

Be honest. You haven't even made a cat video yet, have you? Slacker! Respect the art form.

4

Your video becomes a cult classic among five drunk community college kids in Ottumwa, Iowa.

1

Pooping in the litter box isn't really a special talent. It's tough out there. Porcupines are the next big thing in viral videos.

Let's cut to the chase. Better hire a celebrity cat trainer.

Yes. And you'll be mercilessly stalked by the paparazzi on every trip to the vet.

2

3

6

Look, your cat is getting a little old and pudgy for true Internet fame.

Yes. But celebrity comes at a price. Your feline friend becomes hopelessly addicted to catnip.

5

WHO IS MY CELEBRITY LOVE MATCH?

Mere mortals aren't good enough to date you. Find your true celebrity love.

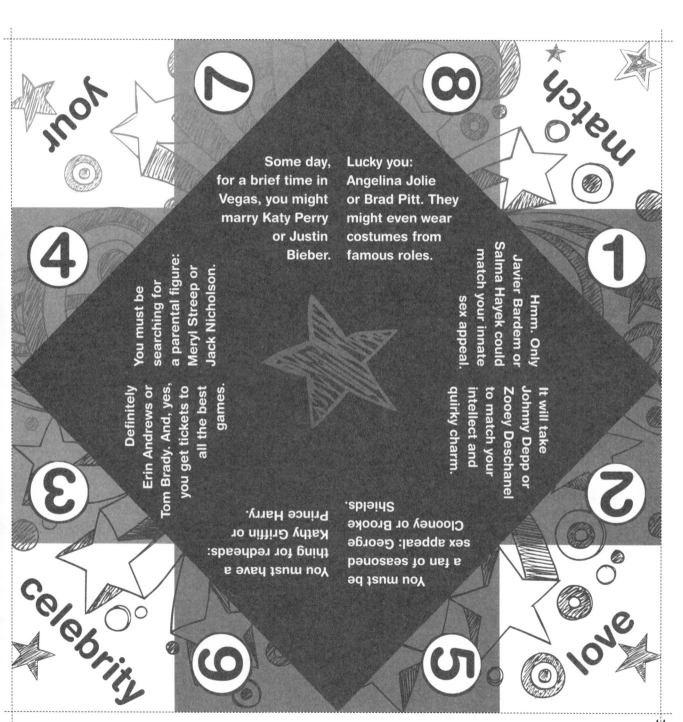

your match celebrity love

7 Some day, for a brief time in Vegas, you might marry Katy Perry or Justin Bieber.

8 Lucky you: Angelina Jolie or Brad Pitt. They might even wear costumes from famous roles.

4 You must be searching for a parental figure: Meryl Streep or Jack Nicholson.

1 Hmm. Only Javier Bardem or Zooey Deschanel could to match your innate sex appeal. It will take Johnny Depp or Salma Hayek to match your intellect and quirky charm.

3 Definitely Erin Andrews or Tom Brady. And, yes, you get tickets to all the best games.

6 You must have a thing for redheads: Kathy Griffin or Prince Harry.

5 You must be a fan of seasoned sex appeal: George Clooney or Brooke Shields.

MAKE YOUR OWN: THE TWO-FACED MONSTER VERSION

Think of it as a pet that doesn't require food, water, or love. Well, maybe a little love.

REAL OR FAKE?

Designer bags. Diamonds. Boobs. Money. Check the authenticity of almost anything.

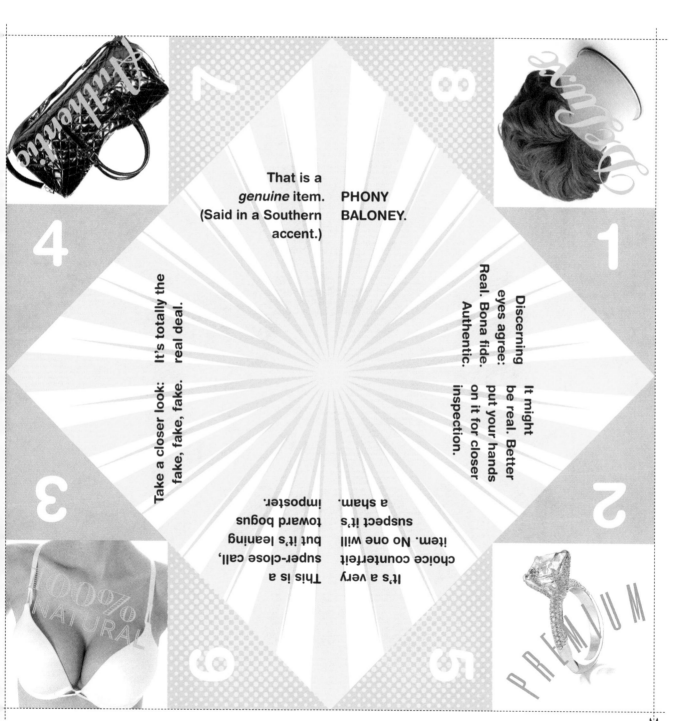

That is a *genuine* item. (Said in a Southern accent.)

PHONY BALONEY.

It's totally the real deal.

Take a closer look: fake, fake, fake.

Discerning eyes agree: Real. Bona fide. Authentic.

It might be real. Better put your hands on it for closer inspection.

This is a super-close call, but it's leaning toward bogus imposter.

It's a very choice counterfeit item. No one will suspect it's a sham.

7

8

4

1

3

2

6

5

WILL I GO TO HELL?

Sure, you might find the answer at church. But this way you can still sleep in on Sunday.

7 H

8

4

1 ⌐

3 E

2

6

5

⌐ L

There's definitely a fire in your future, but you may have just ordered super-spicy Thai food.

If you're worried, try joining one of those free-spirited, anything-goes churches as backup.

Not unless you're planning to go on some horrible crime spree.

Probably. But it's not going to be so bad. All those annoying do-gooders will be in heaven.

No way. I mean, you feel bad when you lie about your weight on your driver's license.

The good news: You're not going to hell. The bad news: Your memoir is going to be a snooze.

Well, you have been hitting some of the Seven Deadly Sins pretty hard: sloth, envy, pride.

Hey, just think of it as an all-expense-paid trip to a fancy sauna. It will be great for your skin.

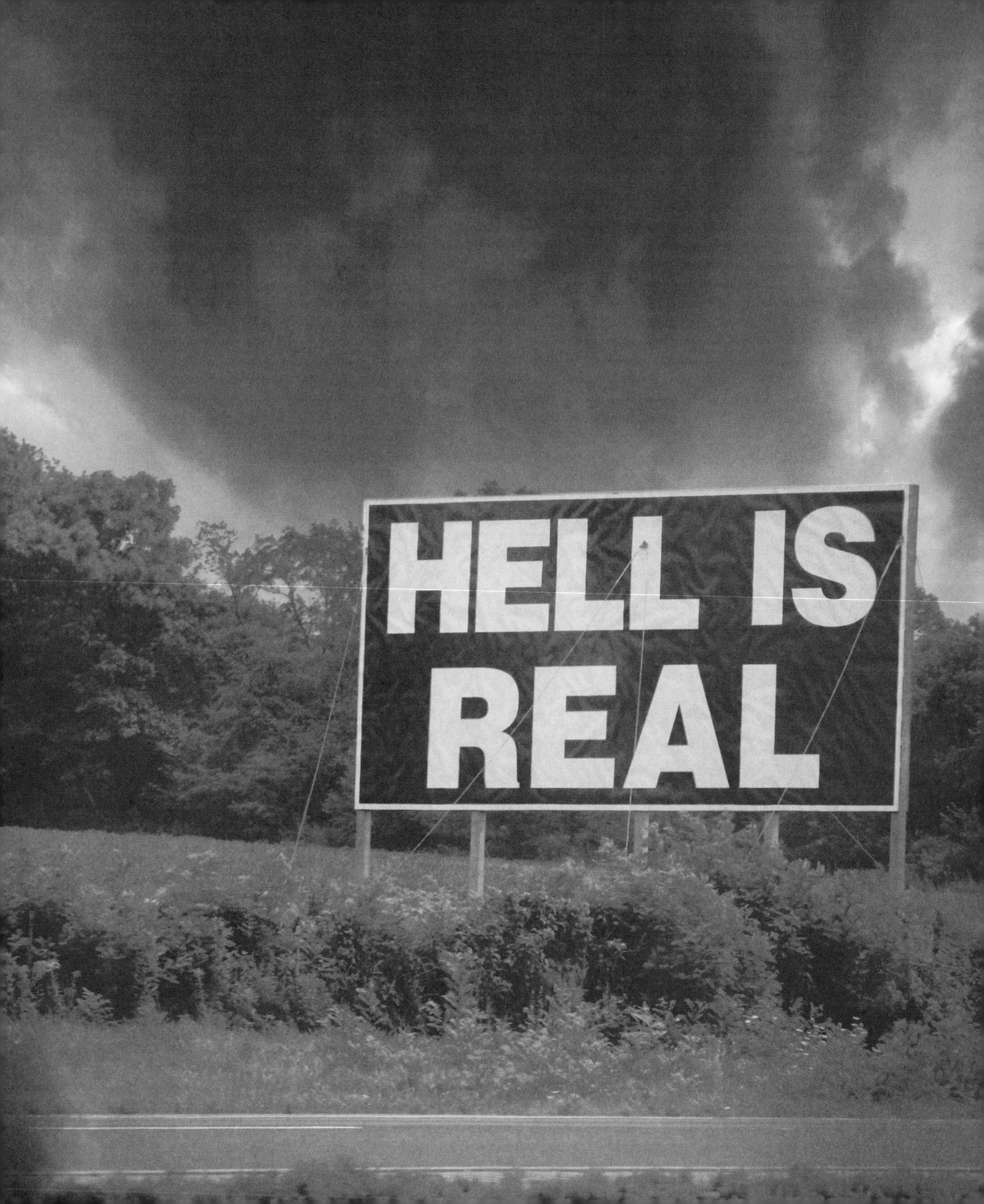
HELL IS
REAL

THE FORTUNE COOKIE COOTIE CATCHER

No need to order takeout. Or eat a stale cookie. Get your Eastern-style wisdom right here.

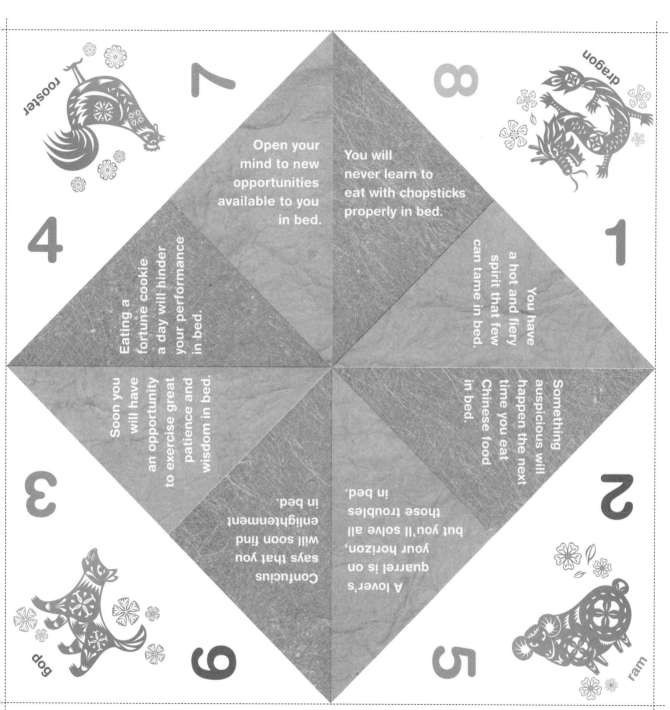

7 rooster

8 dragon

4

1

3 dog

2

6

5 ram

Open your mind to new opportunities available to you in bed.

You will never learn to eat with chopsticks properly in bed.

Eating a fortune cookie a day will hinder your performance in bed.

You have a hot and fiery spirit that few can tame in bed.

Soon you will have an opportunity to exercise great patience and wisdom in bed.

Something auspicious will happen the next time you eat Chinese food in bed.

Confucius says that you will soon find enlightenment in bed.

A lover's quarrel is on your horizon, but you'll solve all those troubles in bed.

WILL I DIE YOUNG?

All the famous rock stars do it. Time to find out if you'll follow in their footsteps.

FRIEND OR FRENEMY?

Will your real friends please stand up? If only it were that easy. Try this friendship litmus test.

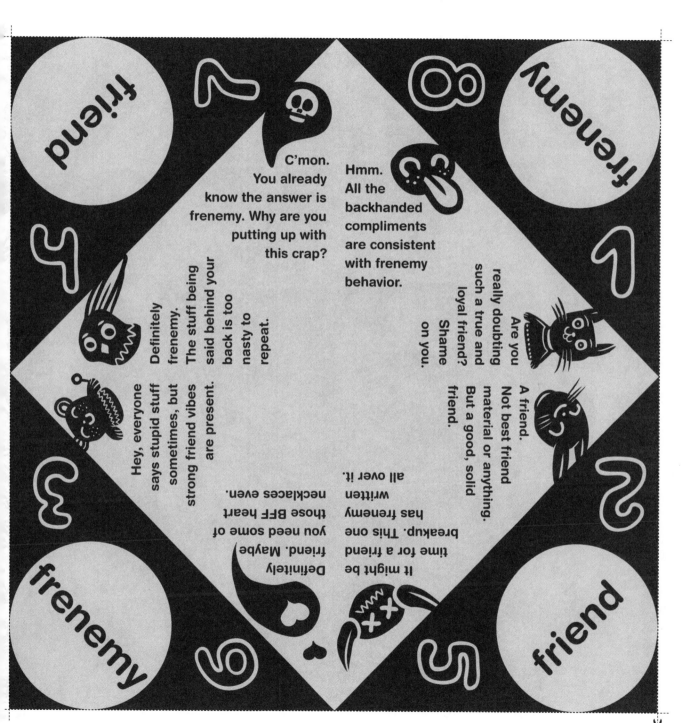

IS IT TIME TO SHAVE MY BEARD?

This is a big decision. Better let this expert fortune-teller weigh in before doing anything rash.

rock 7

it 8

4

1

Go ahead and shave already. It will make your mom really, really happy.

Hmm. You're looking a bit Unabomber-esque. Is that what you're going for?

Keep the beard. It gives you an Abe Lincoln air of wisdom and intellect.

Time to shave. You're scratching your sweetie during make-out sessions. Also, it keeps your face warm.

Three-day stubble is way sexier than a beard. Start a sporadic shaving program.

Rock it. That beard is part of your signature style. Also, it keeps your face warm.

3

2

Ditch the beard, but please keep that super-steamy mustache going, OK?

Better hang on to the beard. Everyone digs that mountain-man look you've been rocking.

or 6

shave 5

AM I BEING FOLLOWED?

Some might call you paranoid. But let's consult this cootie catcher before rushing to conclusions.

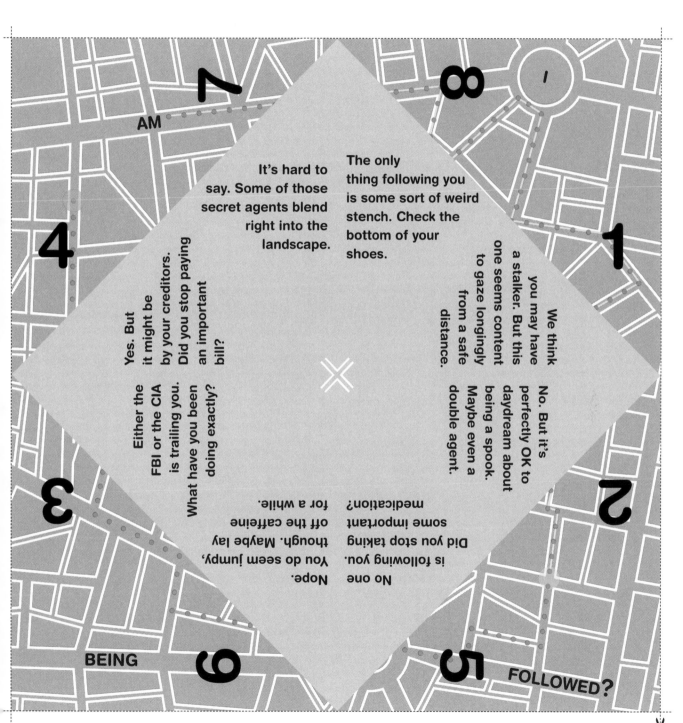

AM

BEING

FOLLOWED?

It's hard to say. Some of those secret agents blend right into the landscape.

The only thing following you is some sort of weird stench. Check the bottom of your shoes.

Yes. But it might be by your creditors. Did you stop paying an important bill?

We think you may have a stalker. But this one seems content to gaze longingly from a safe distance.

No. But it's perfectly OK to daydream about being a spook. Maybe even a double agent.

Either the FBI or the CIA is trailing you. What have you been doing exactly?

Nope. You do seem jumpy, though. Maybe lay off the caffeine for a while.

No one is following you. Did you stop taking some important medication?

MAKE YOUR OWN: THE LET'S CELEBRATE VERSION

It's not a party without a cootie catcher. Fill in the fortunes and celebrate just about anything.

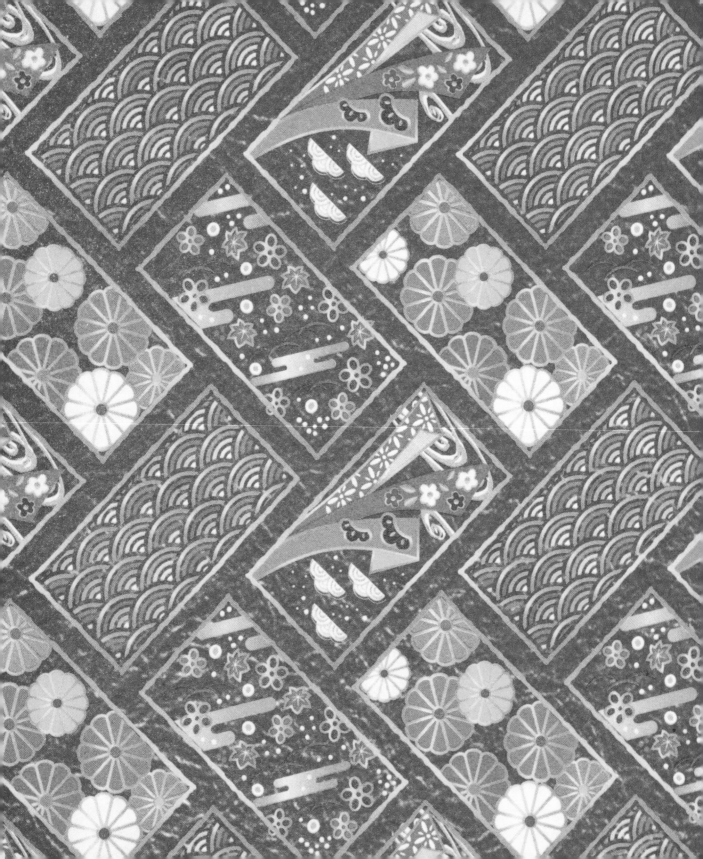

WHAT WOULD MR. T DO?

Lost? Confused? You need a few words of wisdom from Mr. T, the ultimate bad-ass.

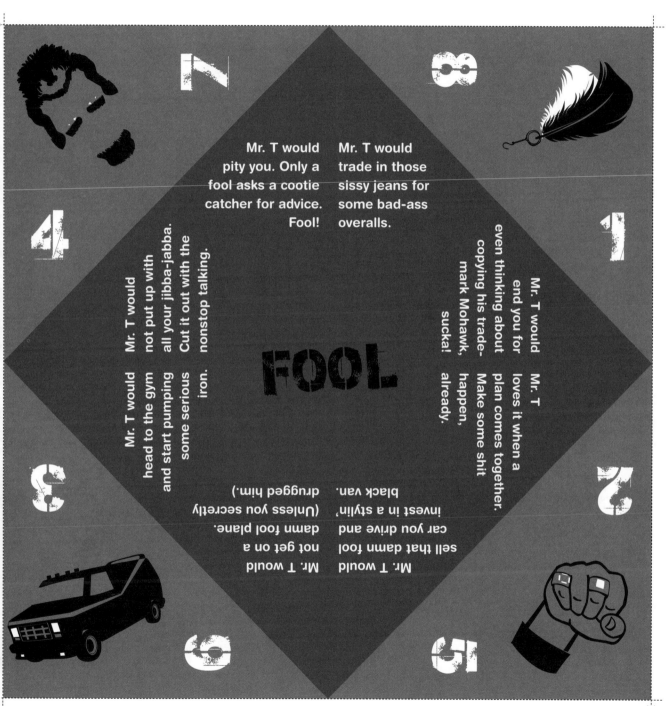

WILL MY NOVEL/ALBUM SELL?

Everyone knows you're talented. Now find out if the powers-that-be will reward your genius.

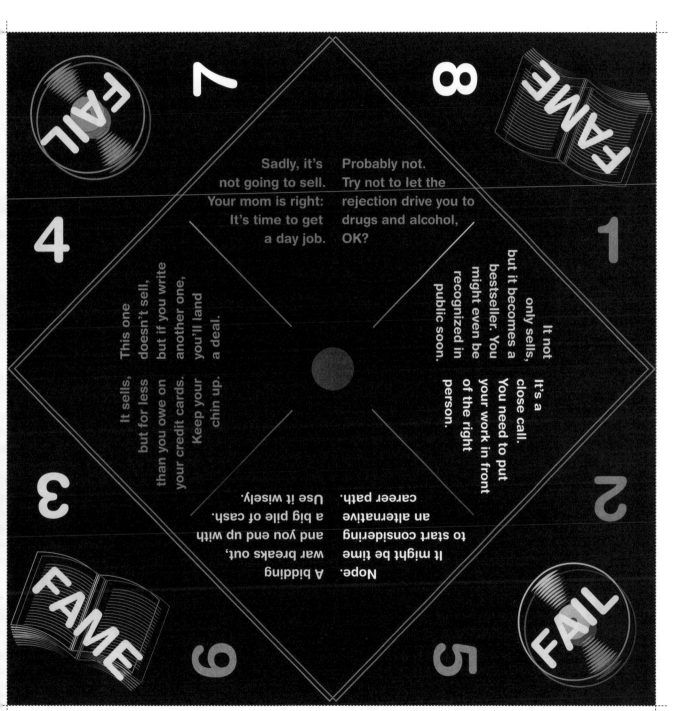

FAIL 7

8 **FAME**

4

Sadly, it's not going to sell. Your mom is right: It's time to get a day job.

Probably not. Try not to let the rejection drive you to drugs and alcohol, OK?

1

This one doesn't sell, but if you write another one, you'll land a deal.

It not only sells, but it becomes a bestseller. You need to put your work in front of the right person. It's a close call. You might even be recognized in public soon.

It sells, but for less than you owe on your credit cards. Keep your chin up.

3

A bidding war breaks out, and you end up with a big pile of cash. Use it wisely.

Nope. It might be time to start considering an alternative career path.

2

FAME 9

5 **FAIL**

WHERE THE F%&K IS MY SOUL MATE?

We have the real answer (unlike those cheery, chipper online dating sites). Find him/her now.

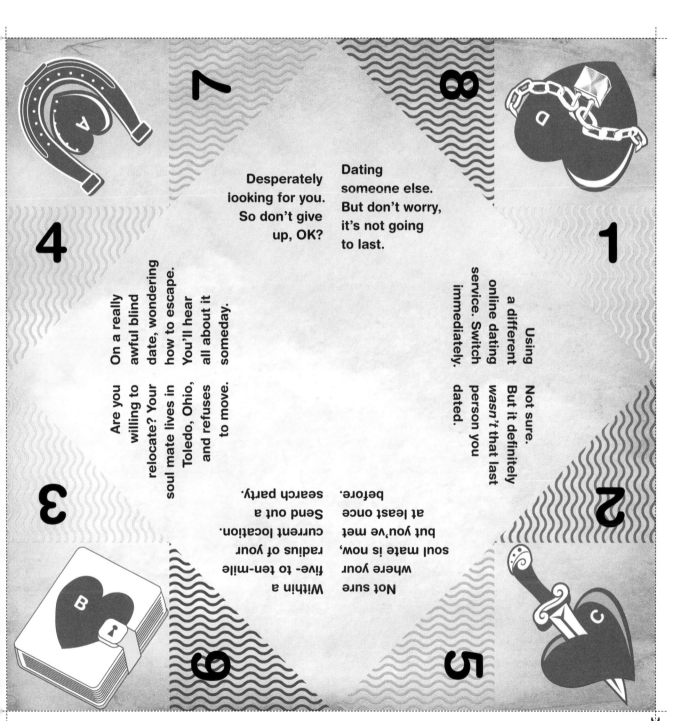

Desperately looking for you. So don't give up, OK?

Dating someone else. But don't worry, it's not going to last.

Using a different online dating service. Switch person you immediately. Not sure. But it definitely *wasn't* that last dated.

On a really awful blind date, wondering how to escape. You'll hear all about it someday.

Are you willing to relocate? Your soul mate lives in Toledo, Ohio, and refuses to move.

Within a five- to ten-mile radius of your current location. Send out a search party.

Not sure where your soul mate is now, but you've met at least once before.

WHAT KIND OF MONSTER AM I?

Illustrated by Stefan G. Bucher

Everyone has an inner monster. But what exactly does yours look like? Find out now with these illustrated fortunes. (Hint: Use the number of eyeballs for game play.)

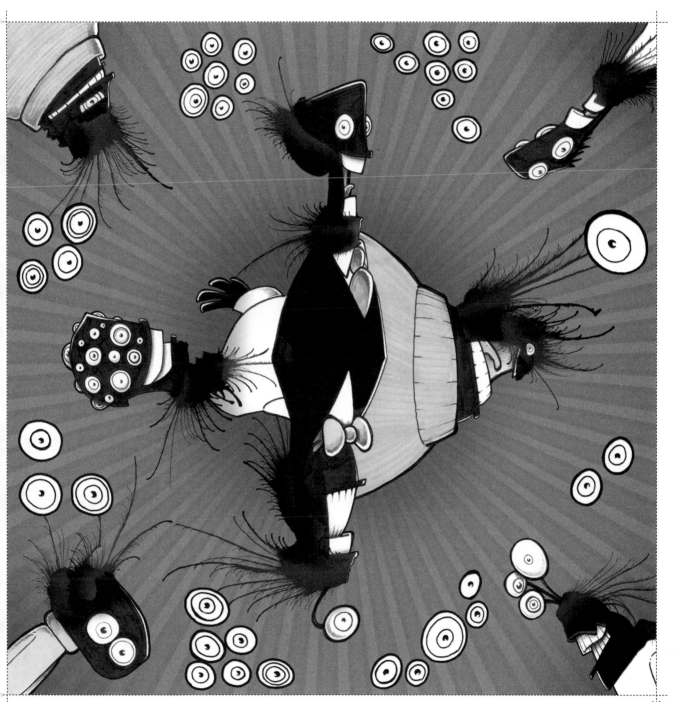

MAKE YOUR OWN: THE BIRTHDAY CARD VERSION

Forgot to buy a card? Write in a few personalized wishes to impress the heck out of friends.

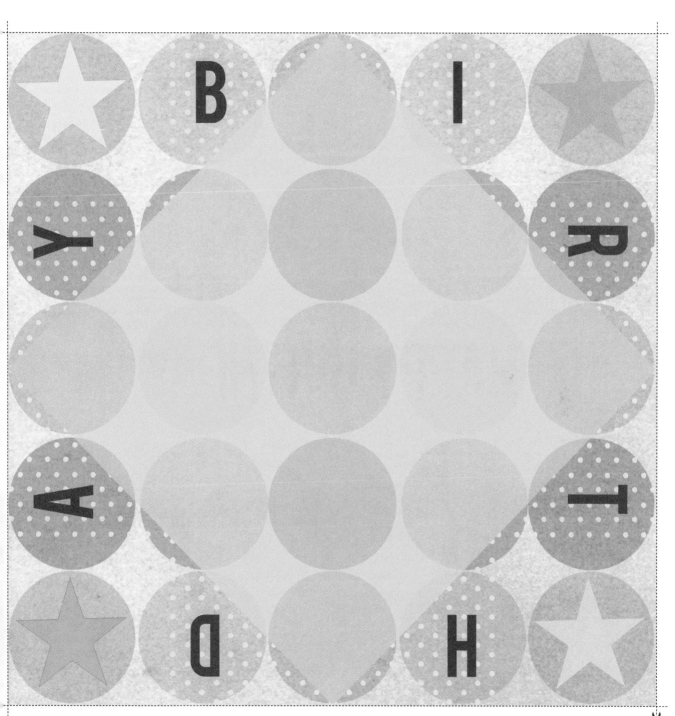

HAPPY BIRTHDAY

WHICH STATEMENT GLASSES ARE FOR ME?

This is a big, big deal. I mean, it's your face for goodness' sakes. Better make the right choice.

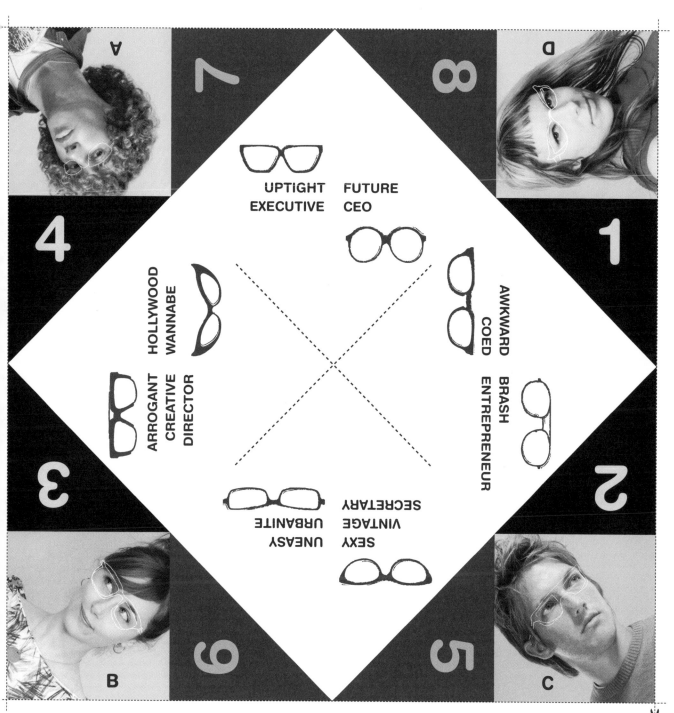

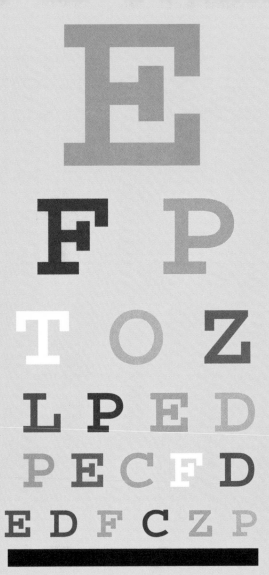

I TOTALLY MESSED UP. PLEASE FORGIVE ME.

Need a really classy way to apologize? Look no further than this paper fortune-teller.

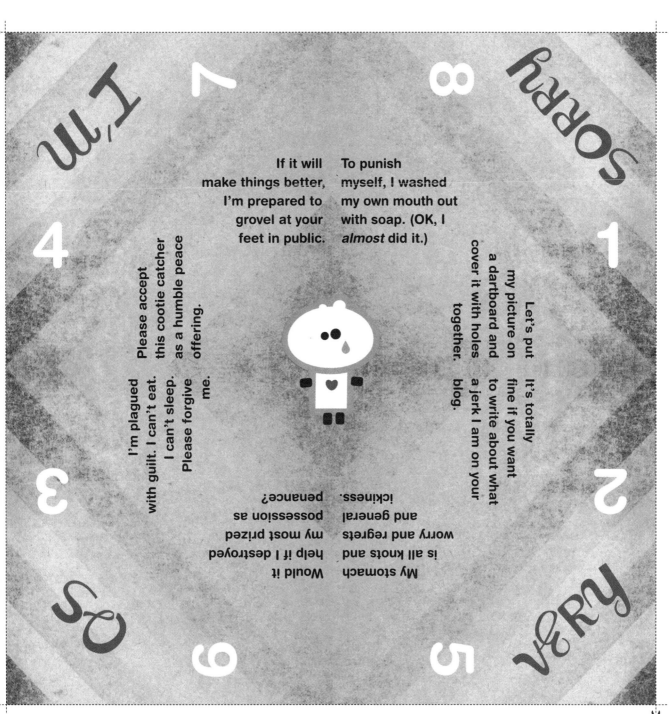

I'M

7

8

SORRY

4

If it will make things better, I'm prepared to grovel at your feet in public.

To punish myself, I washed my own mouth out with soap. (OK, I *almost* did it.)

1

Please accept this cootie catcher as a humble peace offering.

Let's put my picture on a dartboard and cover it with holes.

It's totally fine if you want to write about what a jerk I am on your blog.

3

I'm plagued with guilt. I can't eat. I can't sleep. Please forgive me.

Would it help if I destroyed my most prized possession as penance?

My stomach is all knots and worry and regrets and general ickiness.

2

SO

6

5

VERY

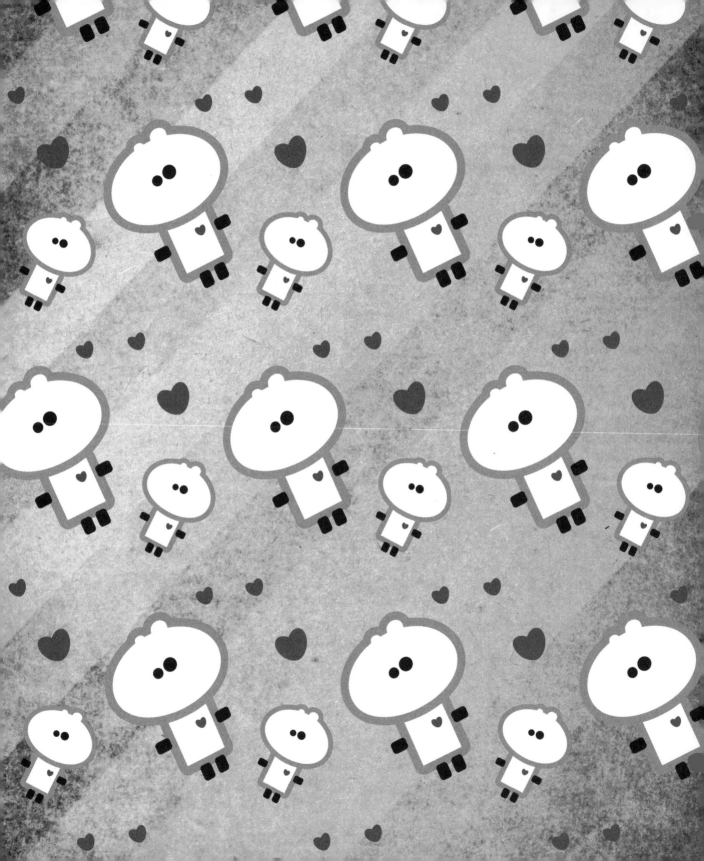

AM I A FASHION VICTIM?

There's a fine line between stylish and laughingstock. Stay on the right side.

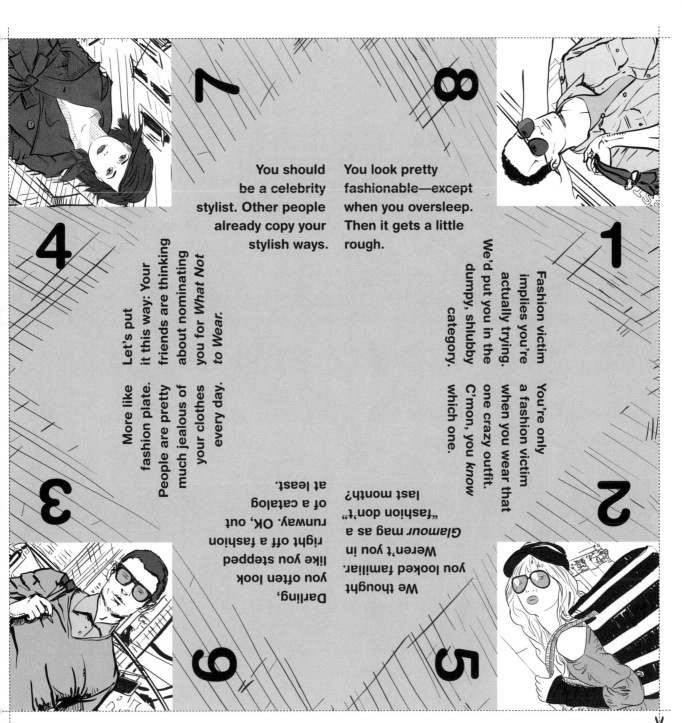

7

8

4

1

You should be a celebrity stylist. Other people already copy your stylish ways.

You look pretty fashionable—except when you oversleep. Then it gets a little rough.

Let's put it this way: Your friends are thinking about nominating you for *What Not to Wear.*

Fashion victim implies you're a fashion victim when you wear that one crazy outfit. We'd put you in the dumpy, shlubby category. C'mon, you *know* which one.

You're only a fashion victim when you wear that one crazy outfit. We'd put you in the dumpy, shlubby category. C'mon, you *know* which one.

More like fashion plate. People are pretty much jealous of your clothes every day.

Darling, you often look like you stepped right off a fashion runway. OK, out of a catalog at least.

We thought you looked familiar. Weren't you in *Glamour* mag as a "fashion don't" last month?

3

6

5

2

WILL YOU MARRY ME?

So, you're ready to pop the big question. Do it in style with this paper fortune-teller.

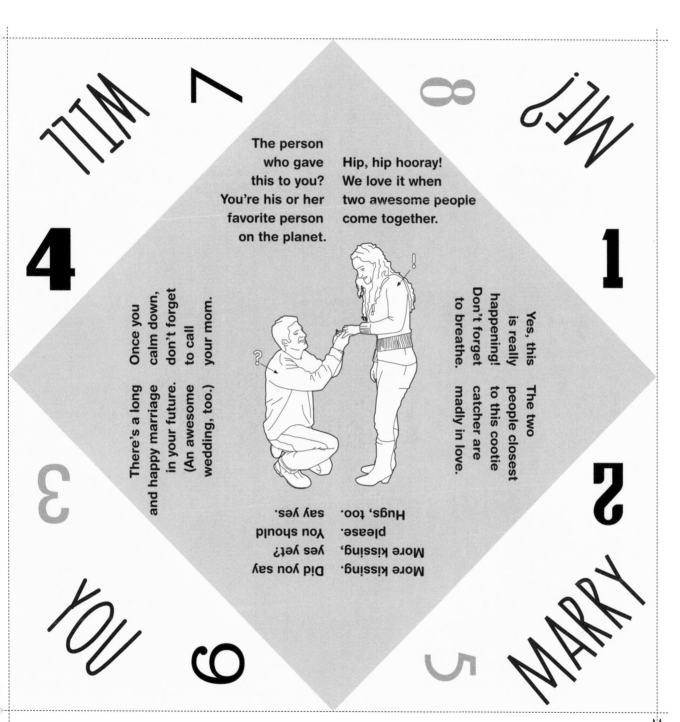

WILL

MR?

7

8

4

1

The person who gave this to you? You're his or her favorite person on the planet.

Hip, hip hooray! We love it when two awesome people come together.

Once you calm down, don't forget to call your mom.

There's a long and happy marriage in your future. (An awesome wedding, too.)

Yes, this is really happening! Don't forget to breathe.

The two people closest to this cootie catcher are madly in love.

More kissing. Hugs, too.

More kissing, please.

Did you say yes yet? You should say yes.

3

2

YOU

MARRY

6

5

HAPPILY EVER AFTER

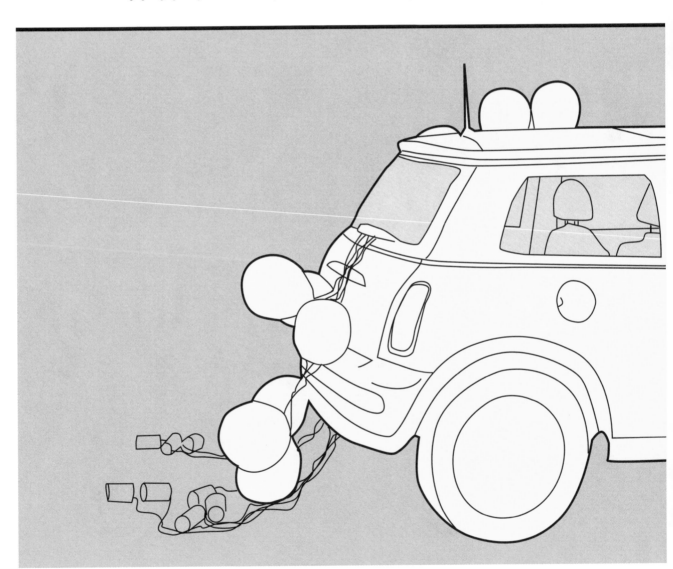

WHAT WOULD CLEOPATRA DO?

Beauty, brains, power, and A-list lovers. Start living like an Egyptian queen right now.

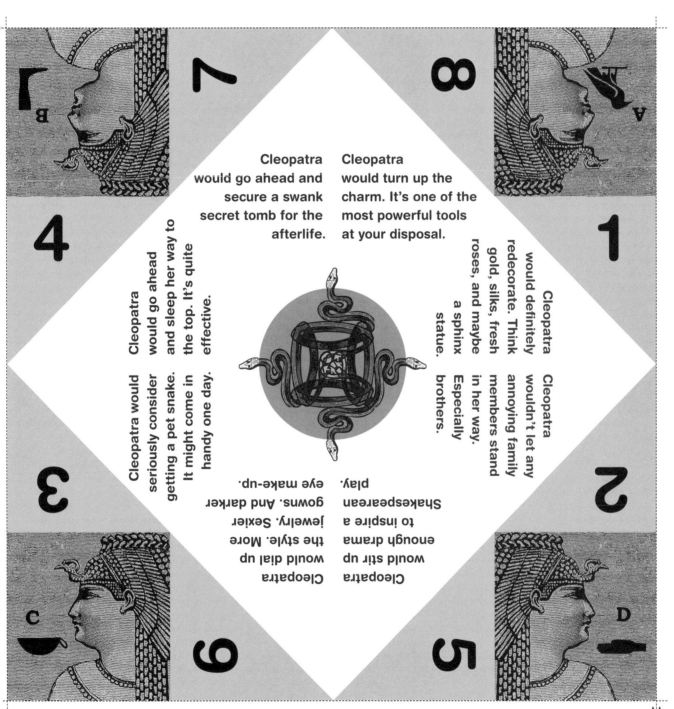

Cleopatra would go ahead and secure a swank secret tomb for the afterlife.

Cleopatra would turn up the charm. It's one of the most powerful tools at your disposal.

Cleopatra would definitely redecorate. Think gold, silks, fresh roses, and maybe a sphinx statue.

Cleopatra wouldn't let any annoying family members stand in her way. Especially brothers.

Cleopatra would go ahead and sleep her way to the top. It's quite effective.

Cleopatra would seriously consider getting a pet snake. It might come in handy one day.

Cleopatra would dial up the style. More jewelry. Sexier gowns. And darker eye make-up.

Cleopatra would stir up enough drama to inspire a Shakespearean play.

SO I'M TURNING 21

Words of wisdom and celebration to make it through this day without mortal injury.

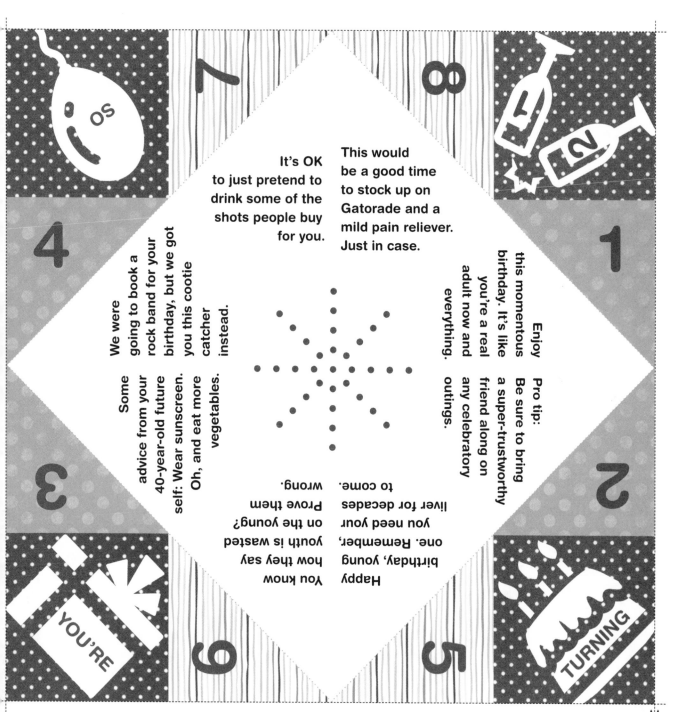

It's OK to just pretend to drink some of the shots people buy for you.

This would be a good time to stock up on Gatorade and a mild pain reliever. Just in case.

We were going to book a rock band for your birthday, but we got you this cootie catcher instead.

Enjoy this momentous birthday. It's like you're a real adult now and any celebratory outings.

Pro tip: Be sure to bring a super-trustworthy friend along on everything.

Some advice from your 40-year-old future self: Wear sunscreen. Oh, and eat more vegetables.

You know how they say youth is wasted on the young? Prove them wrong.

Happy birthday, young one. Remember, you need your liver for decades to come.

YOU'RE

TURNING

SO

21

MY REALITY TV FATE

Sure, it's easy to play couch potato quarterback. But what if you really made it onto reality TV?

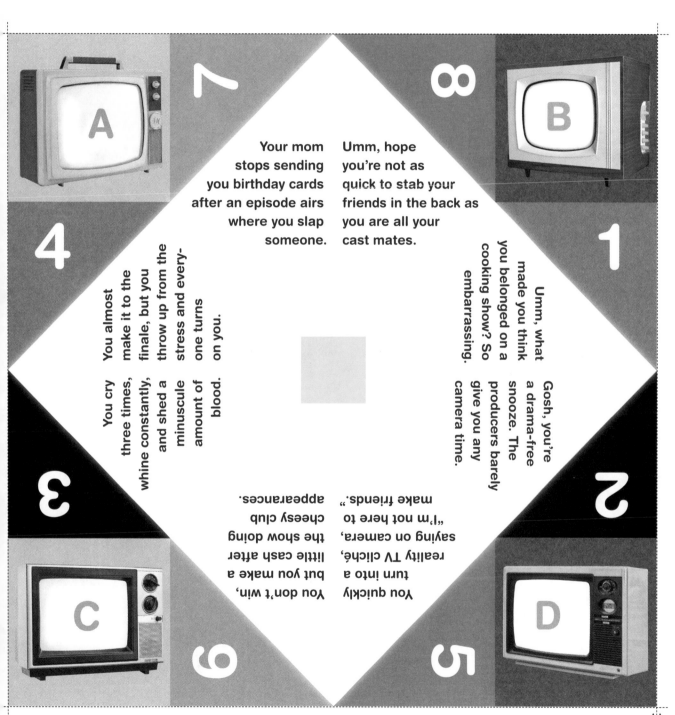

Your mom stops sending you birthday cards after an episode airs where you slap someone.

Umm, hope you're not as quick to stab your friends in the back as you are all your cast mates.

You almost make it to the finale, but you throw up from the stress and everyone turns on you.

You cry three times, whine constantly, and shed a minuscule amount of blood.

Umm, what made you think you belonged on a cooking show? So embarrassing.

Gosh, you're a drama-free snooze. The producers barely give you any camera time.

You don't win, but you make a little cash after the show doing cheesy club appearances.

You quickly turn into a reality TV cliché, saying on camera, "I'm not here to make friends."

WOULD I MAKE IT AS A GRAFFITI ARTIST?

Illustrated by Ed Roth

Sure, Banksy makes street art look fun, glamorous—even easy. But can you cut it?

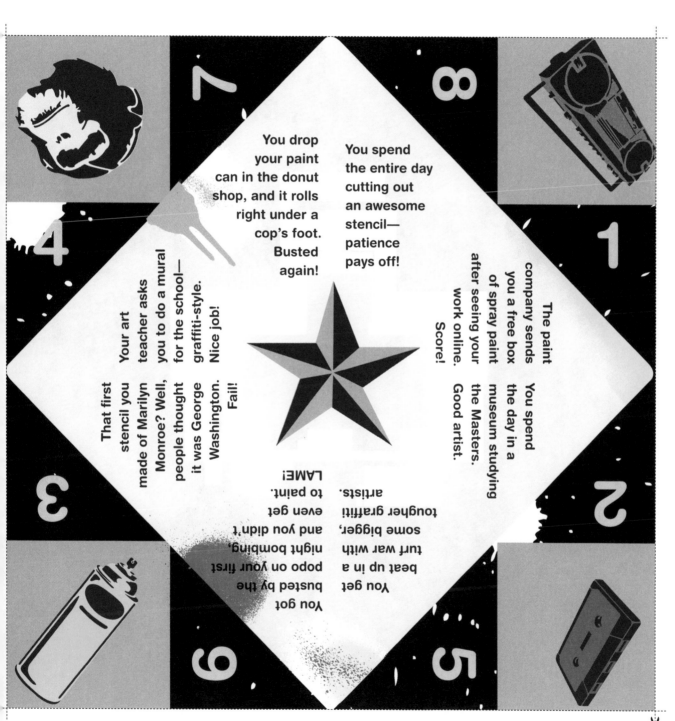

You drop your paint can in the donut shop, and it rolls right under a cop's foot. Busted again!

You spend the entire day cutting out an awesome stencil—patience pays off!

The paint company sends you a free box of spray paint after seeing your work online. Score!

You spend the day in a museum studying the Masters. Good artist.

You get beat up in a turf war with some bigger, tougher graffiti artists.

You got busted by the popo on your first night bombing, and you didn't even get to paint. LAME!

That first stencil you made of Marilyn Monroe? Well, people thought it was George Washington. Fail!

Your art teacher asks you to do a mural for the school—graffiti-style. Nice job!

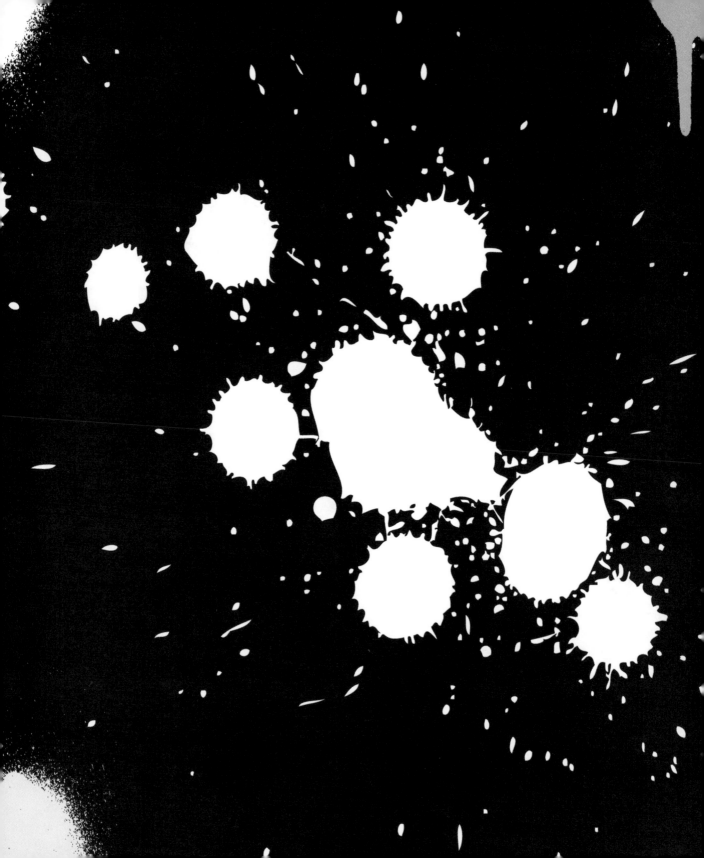

IS THAT VAGUE INTERNET POST ABOUT ME?

So many passive-aggressive people, so little time. Cut through the online crap faster.

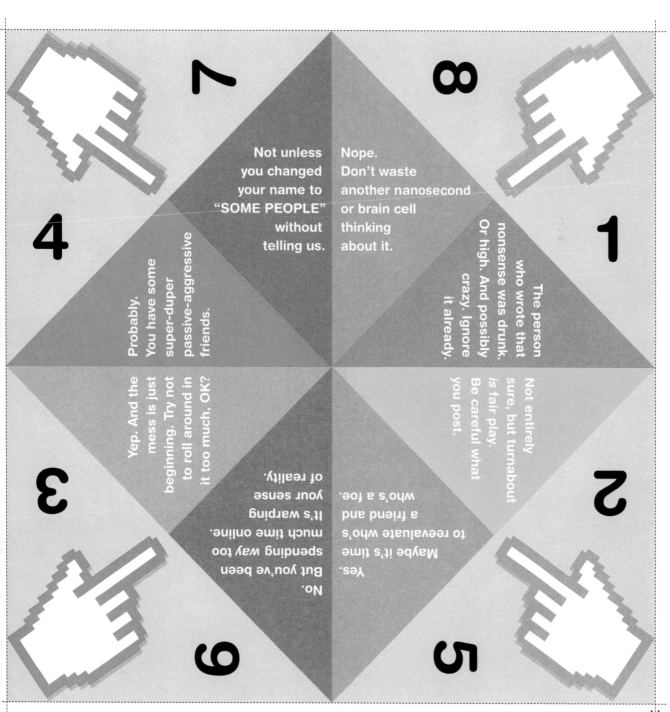

7 — Not unless you changed your name to "SOME PEOPLE" without telling us.

8 — Nope. Don't waste another nanosecond or brain cell thinking about it.

4 — Probably. You have some super-duper passive-aggressive friends.

1 — The person who wrote that nonsense was drunk. Or high. And possibly crazy. Ignore it already.

2 — Not entirely sure, but turnabout is fair play. Be careful what you post.

3 — Yep. And the mess is just beginning. Try not to roll around in it too much, OK?

6 — No. But you've been spending way too much time online. It's warping your sense of reality.

5 — Yes. Maybe it's time to reevaluate who's a friend and who's a foe.

A TALKING CYCLOPS

Stop talking to yourself. Start talking to this lonely, know-it-all Cyclops instead.

AN INSTANT PSYCHIC READING

Who has time to find a reliable psychic, anyway? Here's the lazy person's equivalent.

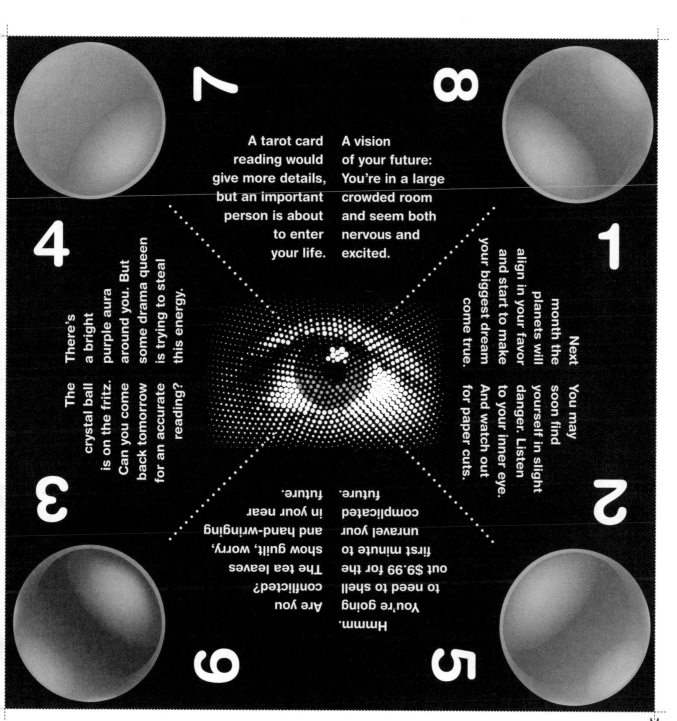

7 A tarot card reading would give more details, but an important person is about to enter your life.

8 A vision of your future: You're in a large crowded room and seem both nervous and excited.

4 There's a bright purple aura around you. But some drama queen is trying to steal this energy.

The crystal ball is on the fritz. Can you come back tomorrow for an accurate reading?

1 Next month the planets will align in your favor and start to make your biggest dream come true. You may soon find yourself in slight danger. Listen to your inner eye. And watch out for paper cuts.

3 Are you conflicted? The tea leaves show guilt, worry, and hand-wringing in your near future.

2 Hmmm. You're going to need to shell out $9.99 for the first minute to unravel your complicated future.

MAKE YOUR OWN: THE SAPPY LOVE NOTE VERSION

Want to score (Brownie points or otherwise)? Just write in heartfelt fortunes for your sweetie.

IS LIVING ALONE MAKING ME PECULIAR?

Illustrated by Aimee Sicuro

You're awesome and independent. But are your quirks starting to freak people out?

Maybe, but it's better to be a little strange than have roommates. They can be the worst.

Not peculiar, exactly. Idiosyncratic seems like the more accurate term.

Only in the most charming way. It's like you're a character in a Neil Gaiman book.

You're not weird. But once in a while, solo living seems to make you a little sad.

You do have that one strange bathroom habit you don't tell anyone about. Best keep it that way. OK?

Just remember to close the door when you're away from home.

Sometimes you give off a crazed "I haven't spoken to another human in three days" vibe.

Couples can be so boring sometimes.

Absolutely not. You're our favorite eccentric.

FORTUNES FOR STRUGGLING ROCK MUSICIANS

Being in the band isn't always what it's cracked up to be. Advice and predictions inside.

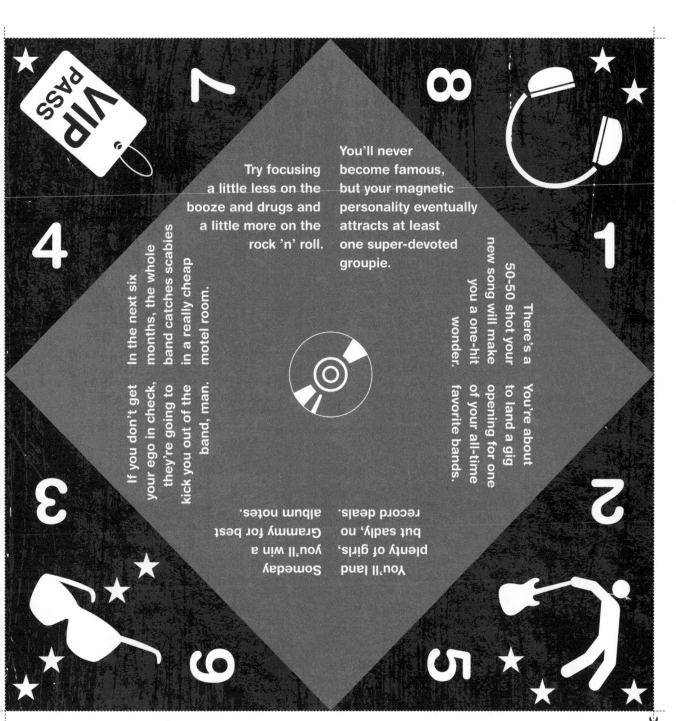

7

8

4

1

Try focusing a little less on the booze and drugs and a little more on the rock 'n' roll.

You'll never become famous, but your magnetic personality eventually attracts at least one super-devoted groupie.

In the next six months, the whole band catches scabies in a really cheap motel room.

There's a 50-50 shot your new song will make you a one-hit wonder.

You're about to land a gig opening for one of your all-time favorite bands.

If you don't get your ego in check, they're going to kick you out of the band, man.

3

2

Someday you'll win a Grammy for best album notes.

You'll land plenty of girls, but sadly, no record deals.

6

5

SHOULD I SAY HI?

You spot someone in public you sort of know. Or sort of hate. Should you start a conversation?

7

should

8

I

Go say hi.
It won't kill you.
And you don't
have to touch
or anything.

**Your call.
The psychic
airwaves are
cautiously optimistic
it will go well if
you do.**

4

1

**No way,
your grooming
habits are too
subpar today for
social contact.**

Yes.
Because if
you don't there
will be angry
tweeting or
blogging about
it later.

Yes.
Not unless
you want to
be stuck in a
long, painful
conversation.

Yes.
It's called
manners. Or simple
human courtesy.
Or having
a heart.

3

2

Well, no.
Not now that
you've been
spotted playing
with a cootie
catcher.

**Don't be
such a big baby.
Go over and say
hello already.**

say

hi?

6

5

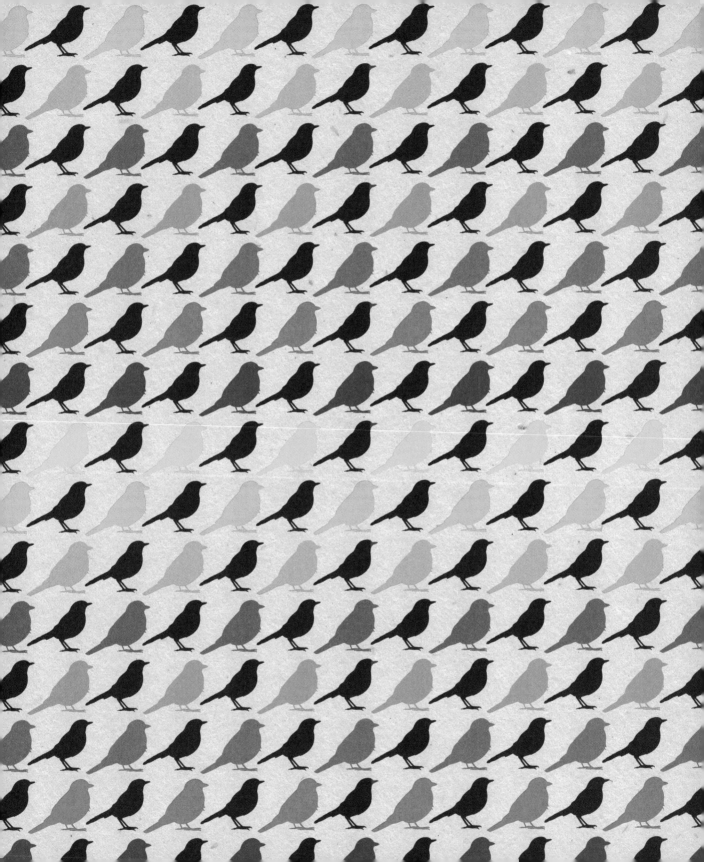

A PRETTY PAPER FLOWER BOUQUET

Real flowers can break the bank. Give anyone a free pick-me-up with this cootie catcher instead.

PRETTY

YOU

Pro tip: Don't water us. It actually makes paper flowers wilt!

The person who gave you these paper flowers thinks you're pretty special.

Unlike most flowers, we become even more beautiful as we age.

Hope these flowers bring a little sunshine—heck, eternal summer—to your day.

If you squint a little, it's kind of like you're in a Monet gorgeous paper painting.

Psst. Everyone else is jealous that some-one gave you this gorgeous paper bouquet.

If you come really close, you can almost smell the roses.

You deserve to have gorgeous flowers around all the time.

FLOWERS

FOR

AM I A HOARDER?

It's a slippery, slimy slope from a sink full of dishes to dead animals under newspapers.

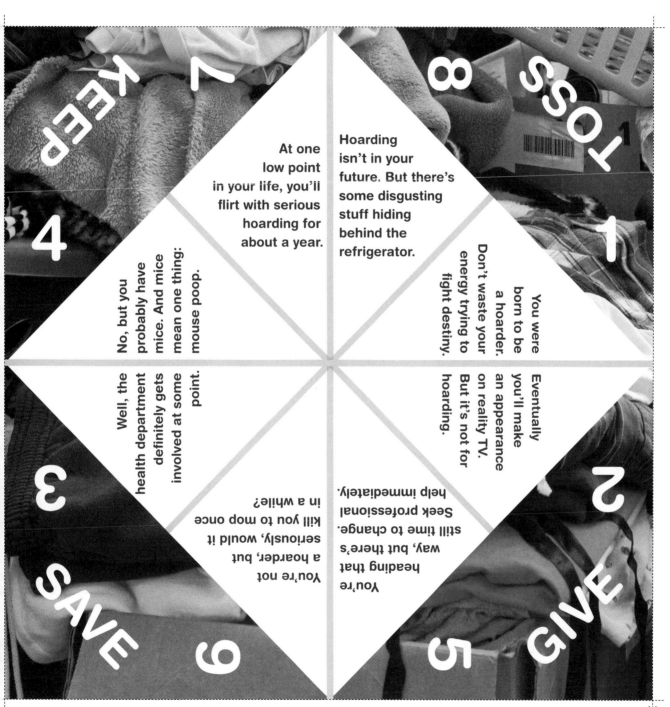

KEEP 7

TOSS 8

4

1

At one low point in your life, you'll flirt with serious hoarding for about a year.

Hoarding isn't in your future. But there's some disgusting stuff hiding behind the refrigerator.

No, but you probably have mice. And mice mean one thing: mouse poop.

You were born to be a hoarder, an appearance on reality TV. Don't waste your energy trying to fight destiny.

Well, the health department definitely gets involved at some point.

Eventually you'll make on reality TV. But it's not for hoarding.

You're not a hoarder, but seriously, would it kill you to mop once in a while?

You're heading that way, but there's still time to change. Seek professional help immediately.

3

SAVE

9

GIVE 5

2

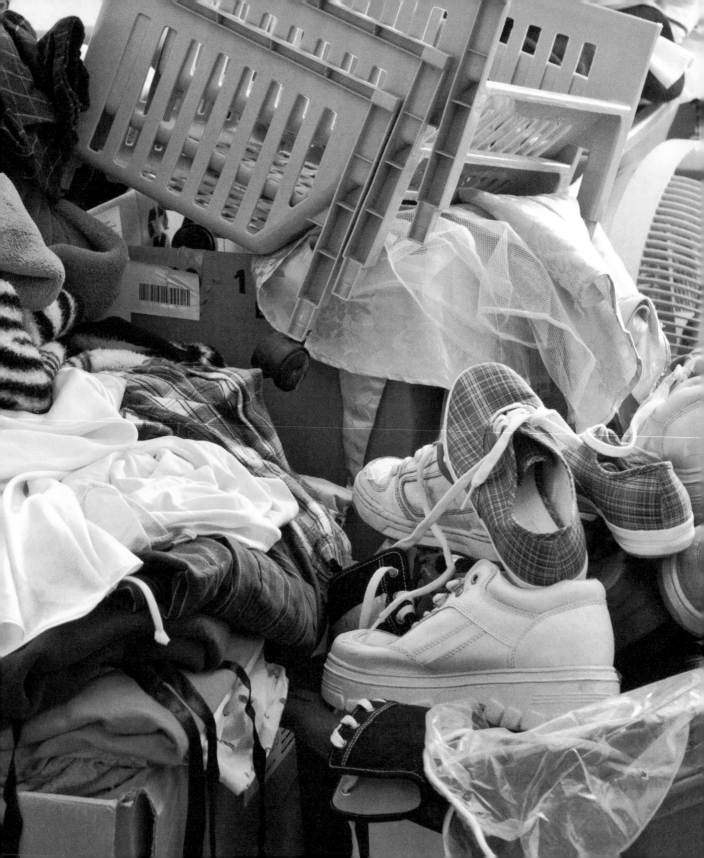

SHOULD I GO SWIMMING?

Come on in, the water is fine. Or is it? Find out if you should jump in the pool.

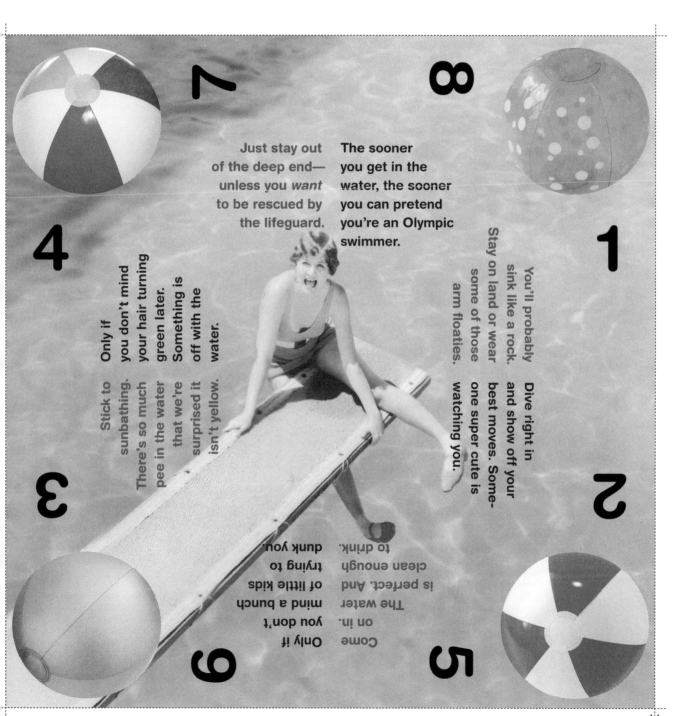

7

8

Just stay out of the deep end— unless you *want* to be rescued by the lifeguard.

The sooner you get in the water, the sooner you can pretend you're an Olympic swimmer.

4

1

Only if you don't mind your hair turning green later. Something is off with the water.

Stick to sunbathing. There's so much pee in the water that we're surprised it isn't yellow.

You'll probably sink like a rock, and show off your best moves. Some-

Stay on land or wear some of those one super cute is

Dive right in and show off your best moves. Some-

arm floaties. watching you.

3

2

Only if you don't mind a bunch of little kids trying to dunk you.

Come on in. The water is perfect. And clean enough to drink.

9

5

ROCK THE BABY SHOWER

Spice things up with this non-cheesy party game. Have guests complete the sentences.

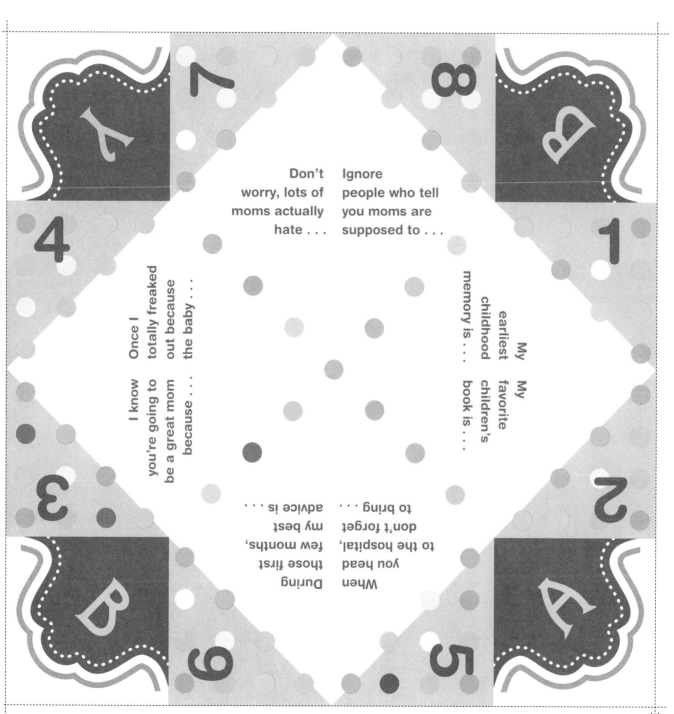

Don't worry, lots of moms actually hate . . .

Ignore people who tell you moms are supposed to . . .

Once I totally freaked out because the baby . . .

My earliest childhood memory is . . .

My favorite children's book is . . .

I know you're going to be a great mom because . . .

During those first few months, my best advice is . . .

When you head to the hospital, don't forget to bring . . .

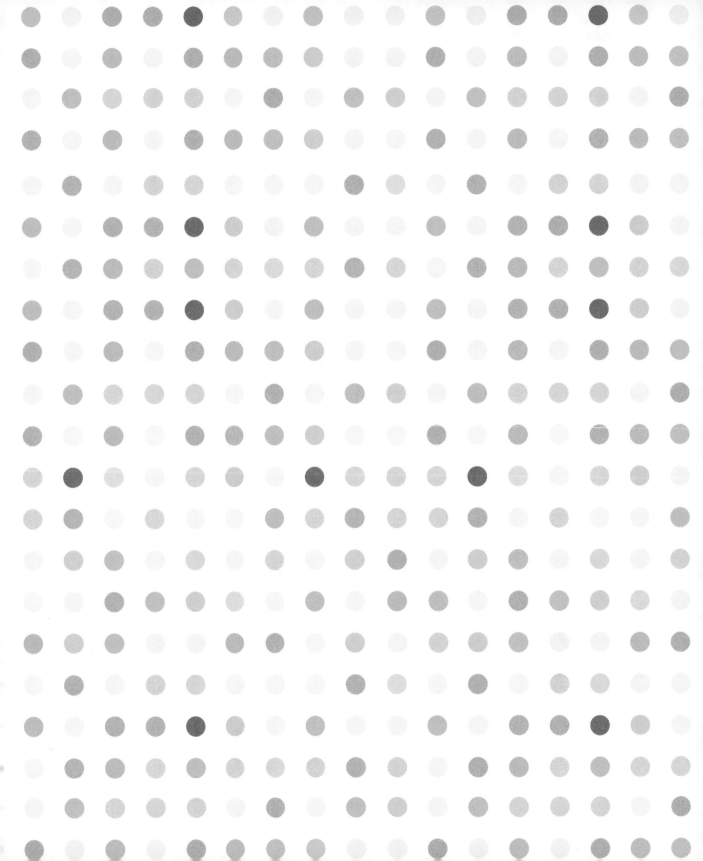

MAKE YOUR OWN: TRUTH OR DARE?

Liven up any gathering with this cootie catcher. Write in your own probing questions and dares.

SHOULD I HAVE ANOTHER COCKTAIL?

Illustrated by Katy Fischer

So many cocktails, so little time. It's hard to know when to cut yourself off—until now.

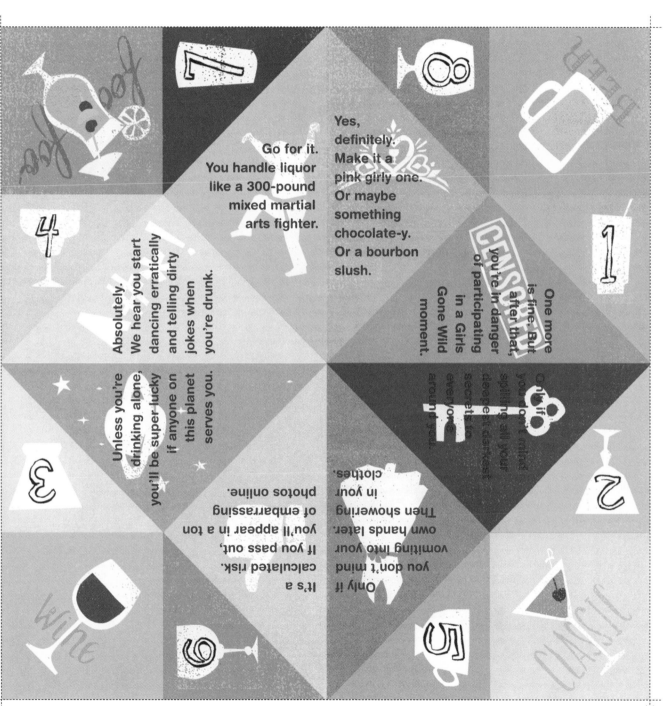

Go for it. You handle liquor like a 300-pound mixed martial arts fighter.

Yes, definitely. Make it a pink girly one. Or maybe something chocolate-y. Or a bourbon slush.

Absolutely. We hear you start dancing erratically and telling dirty jokes when you're drunk.

One more is fine. But after that, you're in danger of participating in a Girls Gone Wild moment.

CENSORED

Only if you don't mind spilling all your deepest darkest secrets to everyone around you.

Unless you're drinking alone, you'll be super-lucky if anyone on this planet serves you.

It's a calculated risk. If you pass out, you'll appear in a ton of embarrassing photos online.

Only if you don't mind vomiting into your own hands later. Then showering in your clothes.

DOES SANTA THINK I'M NAUGHTY OR NICE?

Your gift list is long, but are you on Santa's good side or bad? Find out where you stand.

naughty

nice

7

8

4

1

You're so nice that Santa is starting to suspect that you're hiding something.

Very, very naughty. Santa might leave dog poop in your stocking instead of coal.

Even Santa's reindeer think you're nice. Did you bribe them with carrots?

He knows you've been bad. Sending Mrs. Claus a letter is your only hope.

You're so nice the elves are running short on gossip this year.

Santa thinks you're a little naughty, but he'll probably overlook it.

3

2

naughty

nice

9

5

You're flirting with naughty, but there's still time to reform.

We can't wait to see what Santa brings you.

Super, extra nice.

I'M QUITTING THIS JOB (WITH THIS COOTIE CATCHER)

An awful job requires a dramatic exit. Just leave this on your boss's desk or use it to choose your departing words.

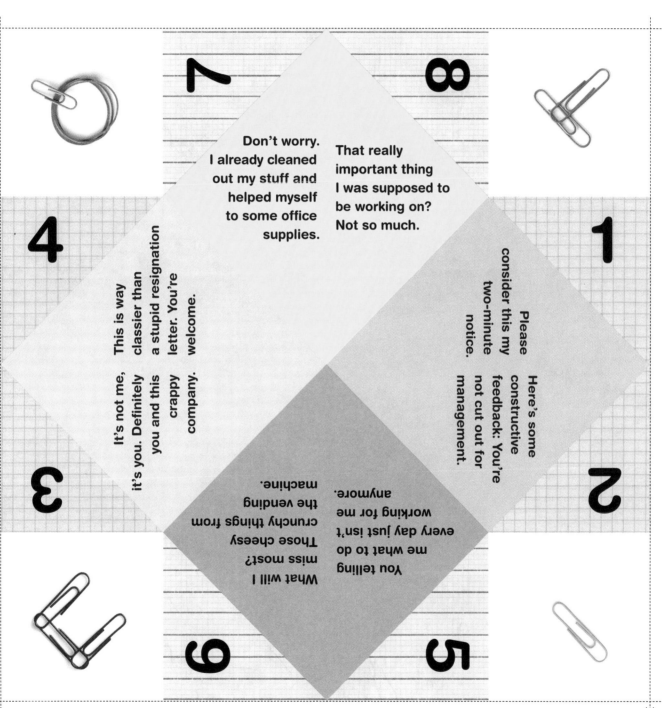

TATTOOS AND ME

So you're a tattoo virgin, eh? Here's a look into your tatted-up—or not so much—future.

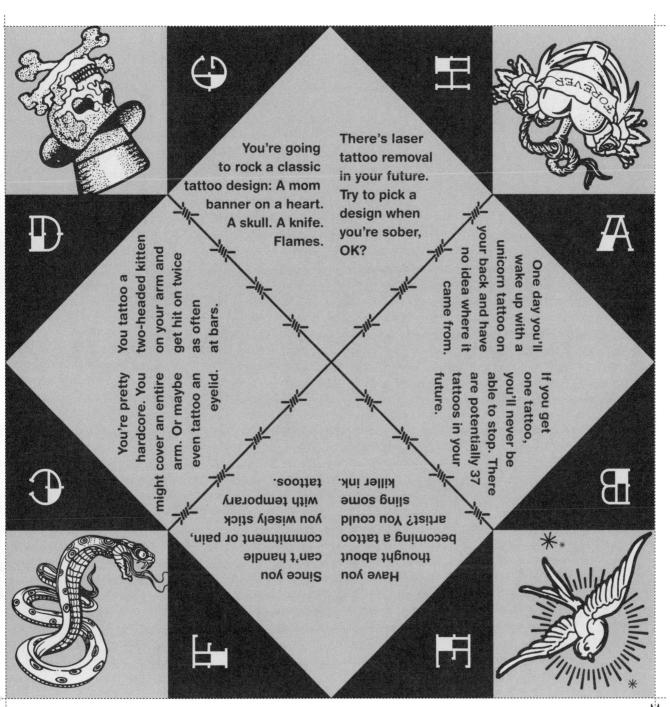

G

H

D

A

C

B

F

E

You're going to rock a classic tattoo design: A mom banner on a heart. A skull. A knife. Flames.

There's laser tattoo removal in your future. Try to pick a design when you're sober, OK?

You tattoo a two-headed kitten on your arm and get hit on twice as often at bars.

One day you'll wake up with a unicorn tattoo on your back and have no idea where it came from.

You're pretty hardcore. You might cover an entire arm. Or maybe even tattoo an eyelid.

If you get one tattoo, you'll never be able to stop. There are potentially 37 tattoos in your future.

Since you can't handle commitment or pain, you wisely stick with temporary tattoos.

Have you thought about becoming a tattoo artist? You could sling some killer ink.

FLING OR RELATIONSHIP MATERIAL?

Oh, sure, the sex is good. But don't waste 18 months dating someone who's *only* hot.

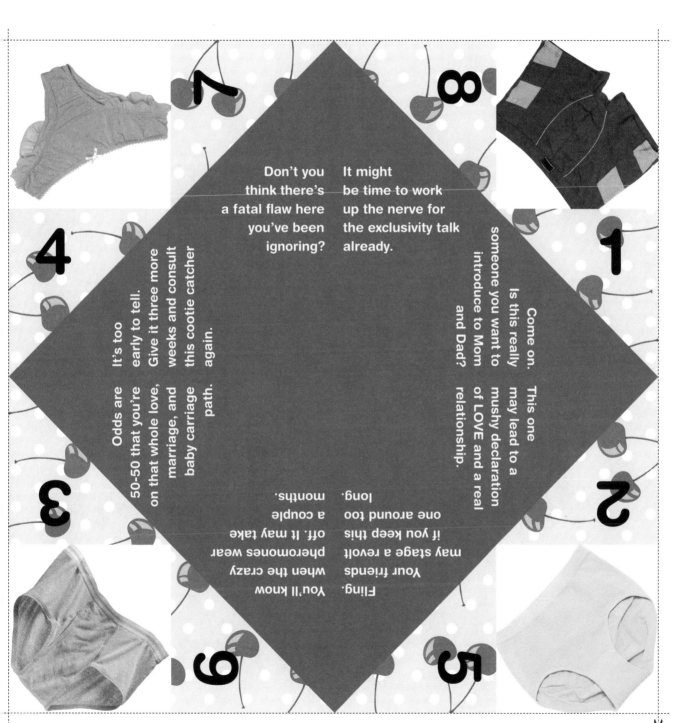

Don't you think there's a fatal flaw here you've been ignoring?

It might be time to work up the nerve for the exclusivity talk already.

Come on. This one may lead to a someone you want to mushy declaration introduce to Mom of LOVE and a real and Dad? relationship.

It's too early to tell. Give it three more weeks and consult this cootie catcher again.

Odds are 50-50 that you're on that whole love, marriage, and baby carriage path.

You'll know when the crazy pheromones wear off. It may take a couple months.

Fling. Your friends may stage a revolt if you keep this one around too long.

WILL I DO JAIL TIME?

The slammer. The pokey. The big house. Spending time behind bars might be in your future.

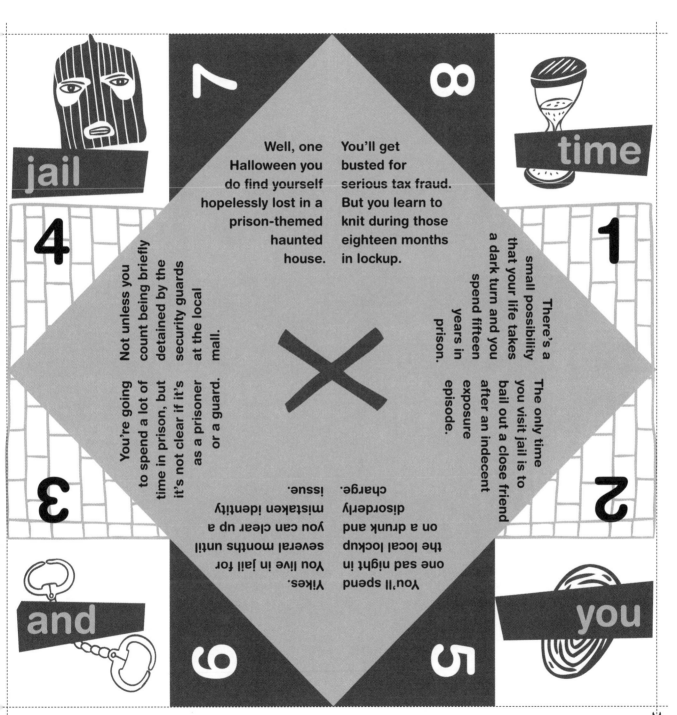

jail

time

and

you

7

8

4

1

3

2

6

5

Well, one Halloween you do find yourself hopelessly lost in a prison-themed haunted house.

You'll get busted for serious tax fraud. But you learn to knit during those eighteen months in lockup.

Not unless you count being briefly detained by the security guards at the local mall.

You're going to spend a lot of time in prison, but it's not clear if it's as a prisoner or a guard.

There's a small possibility that your life takes a dark turn and you spend fifteen years in prison.

The only time you visit jail is to bail out a close friend after an indecent exposure episode.

Yikes. You live in jail for several months until you can clear up a mistaken identity issue.

You'll spend one sad night in the local lockup on a drunk and disorderly charge.

HOW MANY DONUTS CAN I EAT WITHOUT THROWING UP?

So, you fancy yourself a competitive eater. Or maybe just a glutton. Know your hard limits.

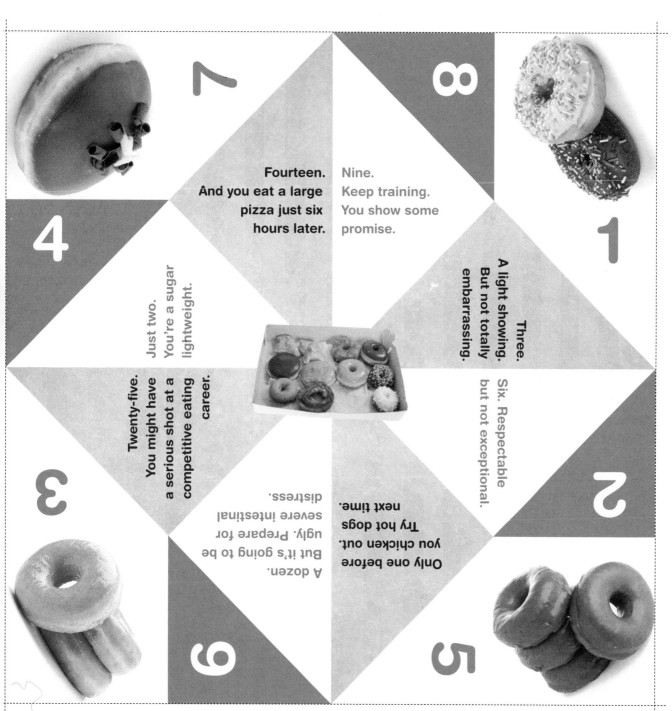

Fourteen. And you eat a large pizza just six hours later.

Nine. Keep training. You show some promise.

Three. A light showing. But not totally embarrassing.

Six. Respectable but not exceptional.

Just two. You're a sugar lightweight.

Twenty-five. You might have a serious shot at a competitive eating career.

A dozen. But it's going to be ugly. Prepare for severe intestinal distress.

Only one before you chicken out. Try hot dogs next time.

MAKE YOUR OWN: A VERY SCARY HALLOWEEN

Illustrated by Noah Scalin

Give these out to trick-or-treaters as is. Or write in freaky fortunes to frighten friends.

FEEL BETTER SUPER SOON

Skip the cheesy, store-bought get well cards. Cheer up a sick friend via cootie catcher.

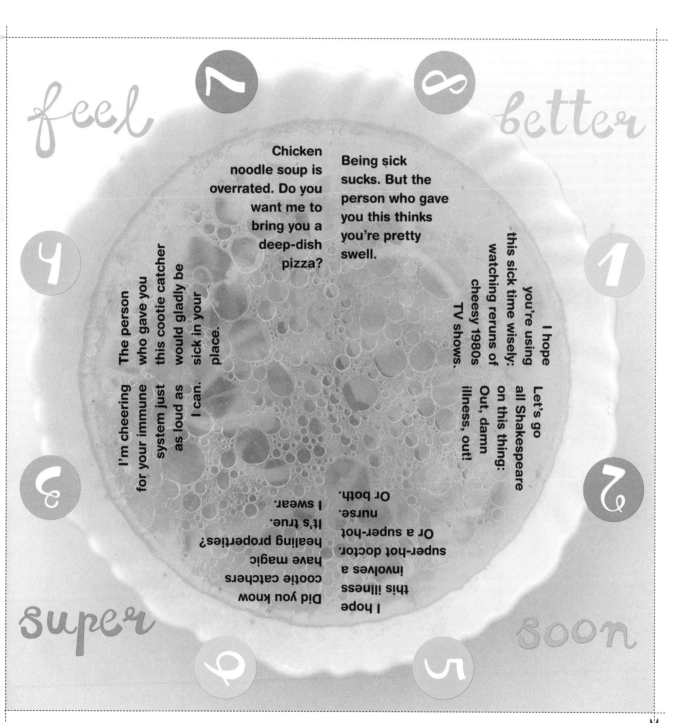

feel

better

super

soon

7

8

4

1

3

2

6

5

Chicken noodle soup is overrated. Do you want me to bring you a deep-dish pizza?

Being sick sucks. But the person who gave you this thinks you're pretty swell.

The person who gave you this cootie catcher would gladly be sick in your place.

I hope you're using this sick time wisely: watching reruns of cheesy 1980s TV shows.

Let's go all Shakespeare on this thing: Out, damn illness, out!

I'm cheering for your immune system just as loud as I can.

Did you know cootie catchers have magic healing properties? It's true. I swear.

I hope this illness involves a super-hot doctor. Or a super-hot nurse. Or both.

THE HIPSTER WEDDING DECORATION

You hate rubbery chicken and Jordan almonds. Give your guests awesome fortunes instead.

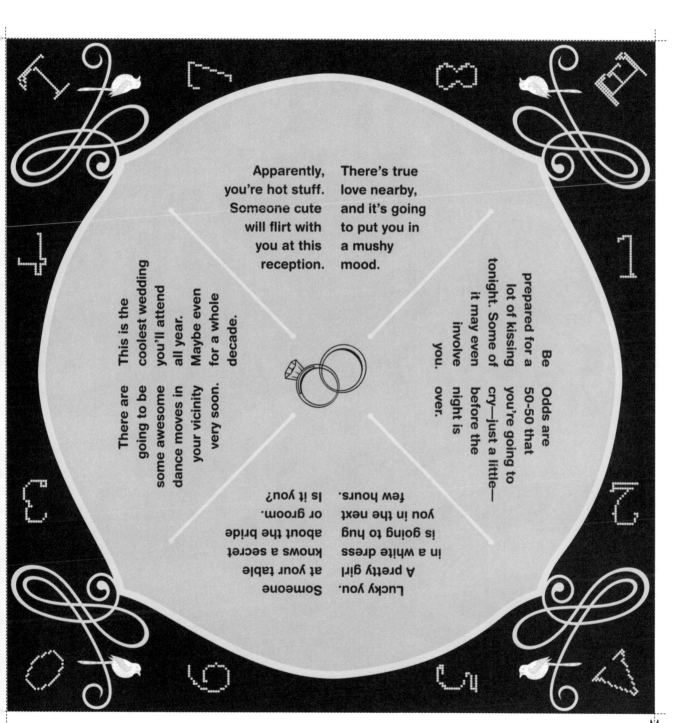

Apparently, you're hot stuff. Someone cute will flirt with you at this reception.

There's true love nearby, and it's going to put you in a mushy mood.

This is the coolest wedding you'll attend all year. Maybe even for a whole decade.

There are going to be some awesome dance moves in your vicinity very soon.

Be prepared for a lot of kissing tonight. Some of it may even involve you.

Odds are 50-50 that you're going to cry—just a little—before the night is over.

Someone at your table knows a secret about the bride or groom. Is it you?

Lucky you. A pretty girl in a white dress is going to hug you in the next few hours.

DID I OVERSHARE?

Yikes, it seems like you just made everyone uncomfortable. But maybe it's all in your head.

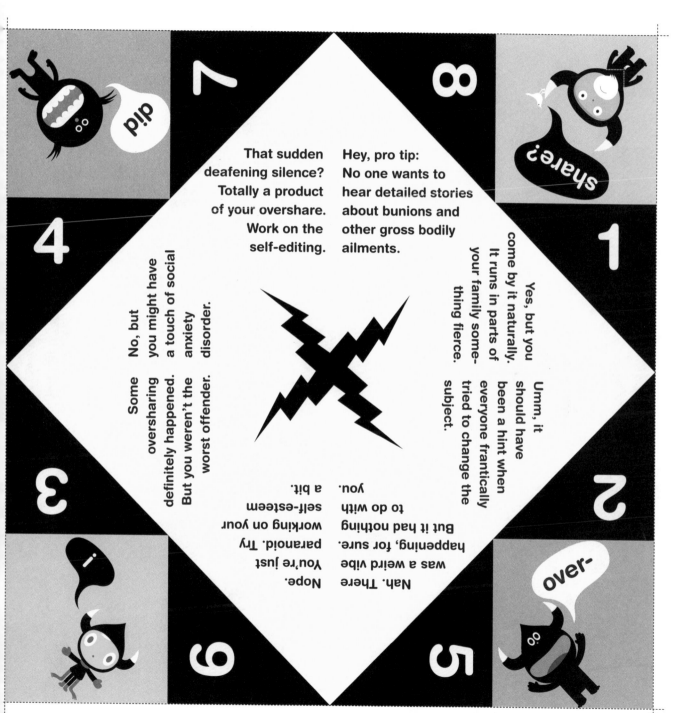

I REALLY, REALLY MISS YOU

Don't bottle up all those special feelings inside. Spread your love via cootie catcher.

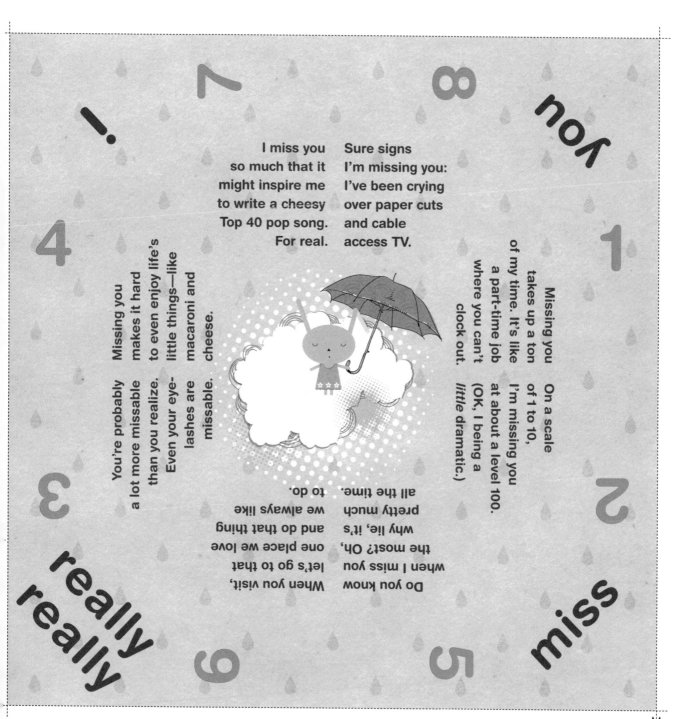

7

8

!

you

4

1

I miss you so much that it might inspire me to write a cheesy Top 40 pop song. For real.

Sure signs I'm missing you: I've been crying over paper cuts and cable access TV.

Missing you takes up a ton of my time. It's like a part-time job where you can't clock out.

On a scale of 1 to 10, I'm missing you at about a level 100. (OK, I being a little dramatic.)

Missing you makes it hard to even enjoy life's little things—like macaroni and cheese.

You're probably a lot more missable than you realize. Even your eyelashes are missable.

3

2

really really

When you visit, let's go to that one place we love and do that thing we always like to do.

Do you know when I miss you the most? Oh, why lie, it's pretty much all the time.

6

5

miss

WOULD I SURVIVE A HORROR MOVIE?

Everyone thinks they'd make it. But do you really live? Or bite it in the first five minutes?

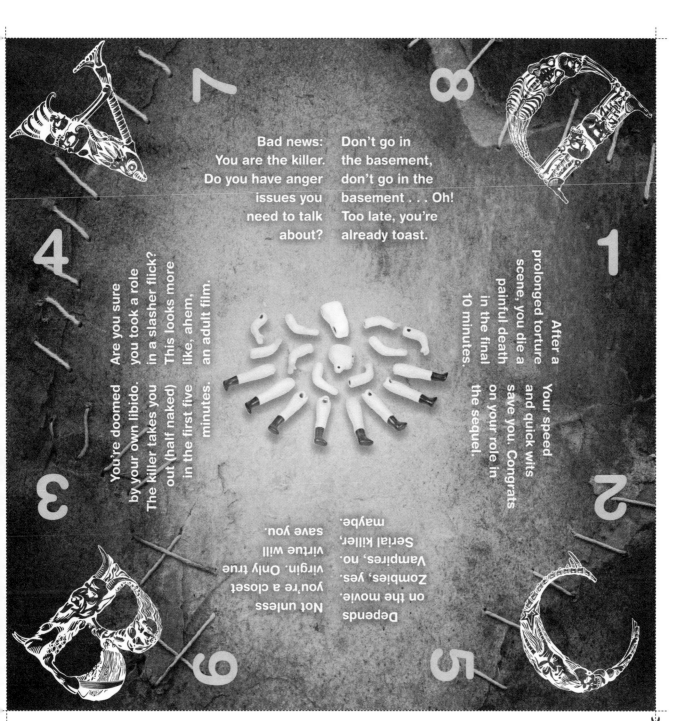

Bad news: You are the killer. Do you have anger issues you need to talk about?

Don't go in the basement, don't go in the basement . . . Oh! Too late, you're already toast.

After a prolonged torture scene, you die a painful death in the final 10 minutes.

Your speed and quick wits save you. Congrats on your role in the sequel.

Are you sure you took a role in a slasher flick? This looks more like, ahem, an adult film.

You're doomed by your own libido. The killer takes you out (half naked) in the first five minutes.

Not unless you're a closet virgin. Only true virtue will save you.

Depends on the movie. Zombies, yes. Vampires, no. Serial killer, maybe.

IMPORTANT MESSAGES FROM MY SUBCONSCIOUS

Discover the deep, deep thoughts skulking about right inside your own skull.

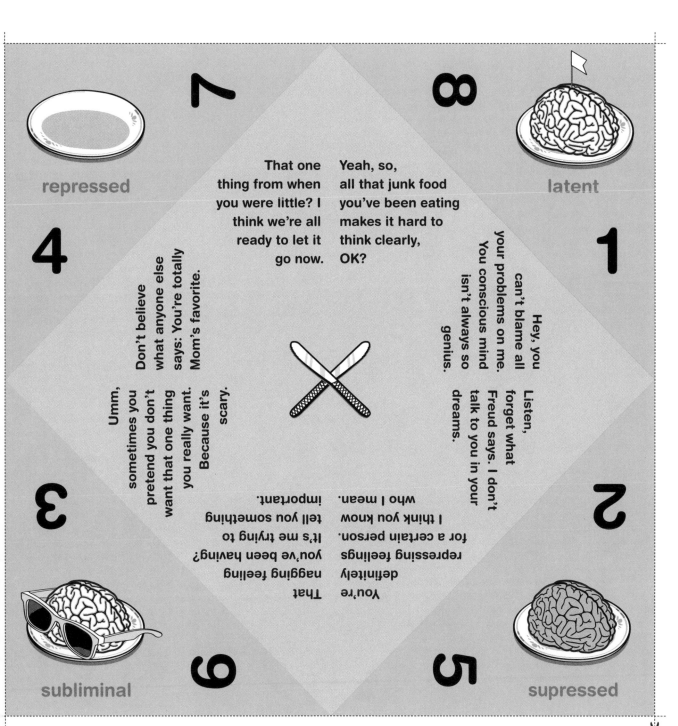

AM I A CYLON?

Illustrated by Ben Patrick

Face the truth: You might be a toaster and not even know it. Just sayin'. It's possible.

WILL ANYONE KISS ME ON NEW YEAR'S EVE?

It's midnight. Tipsy couples all around you start smooching. What about you?

NEW 7

KISS 8

4

1

Choose your footwear wisely. This kiss is going to make you dizzy and weak in the knees.

This isn't your year for kisses and romance. Next year looks really good, though.

How much do you want to be kissed? There's going to be a really creepy person willing.

We're not sure who plants it on you, but prepare yourself for the BEST KISS EVER.

Not unless you lean into the TV screen and plant one on Ryan Seacrest.

A cat or dog is going to lick your face. Does that count?

No kiss. But you'll toast the New Year with some truly fabulous friends.

Only if you're proactive. Start scouting for some hot single lips early in the night.

3 YEAR'S

9

5

EVE 2

WILL I GET PROMOTED?

So, yeah, you'd like a new title and bigger paycheck. Here are your real odds.

WHEN WILL I GET LAID AGAIN?

A bit of a dry spell, eh? No need to fret. This piece of paper reads between the sheets.

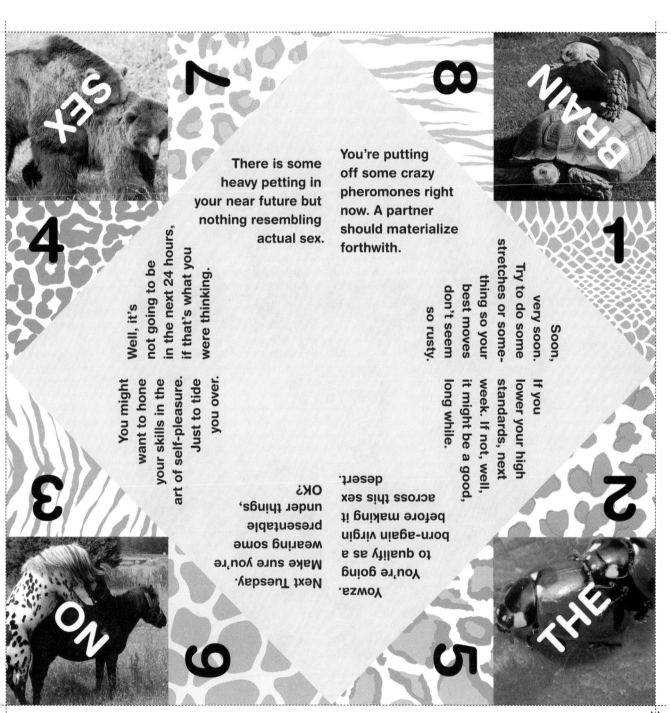

7 SEX

8 BRAIN

4

1

There is some heavy petting in your near future but nothing resembling actual sex.

You're putting off some crazy pheromones right now. A partner should materialize forthwith.

Well, it's not going to be in the next 24 hours, if that's what you were thinking.

Soon, very soon. If you lower your high standards, next week. If not, well, it might be a good, long while. Try to do some stretches or something so your best moves don't seem so rusty.

You might want to hone your skills in the art of self-pleasure. Just to tide you over.

Next Tuesday. Make sure you're wearing some presentable under things, OK?

Yowza. You're going to qualify as a born-again virgin before making it across this sex desert.

3

2

ON

THE

6

5

IS MY DRUNK FRIEND GOING TO VOMIT IN MY CAR?

Being the designated driver comes with certain risks. Manage them with this cootie catcher.

drunk 7

8 friend

4

1

You're in the clear. Proceed with your designated driver duties posthaste.

There's car vomiting. And it's going to smell so bad you almost puke, too.

Your drunk friend vomits three times in thirty minutes. You may never get the odor out of your car.

This is an emergency. Put down this cootie catcher and call your friend a cab.

No vomiting. But your friend yells insults out the window at every passing driver.

Worse. Your friend pukes all over you before you even make it to the car.

3

2

alert 6

5 vomit

It's a close one. But your friend vomits safely in a toilet.

Vomit, check. But, hey, most of it goes out the car window.

IS THERE A SERIAL KILLER IN THE CLOSET?

You're home alone. There's a super-weird noise. It's dark. Better check this shit out.

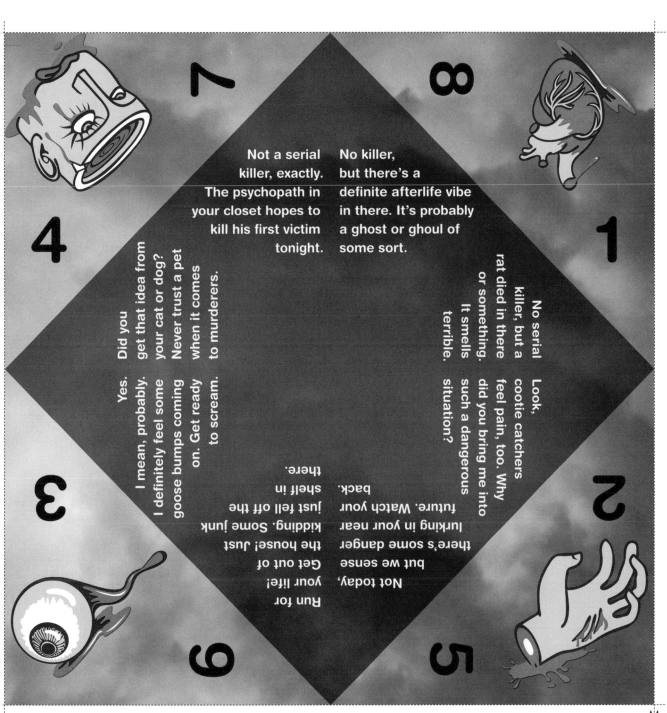

7

8

4

1

Not a serial killer, exactly. The psychopath in your closet hopes to kill his first victim tonight.

No killer, but there's a definite afterlife vibe in there. It's probably a ghost or ghoul of some sort.

Did you get that idea from your cat or dog? Never trust a pet when it comes to murderers.

No serial killer, but a cootie catchers rat died in there feel pain, too. Why or something. did you bring me into It smells such a dangerous terrible. situation?

Yes. I mean, probably. I definitely feel some goose bumps coming on. Get ready to scream.

Run for your life! Get out of the house! Just kidding. Some junk just fell off the shelf in there.

Not today, but we sense there's some danger lurking in your near future. Watch your back.

3

2

6

5

MY PAST LIFE REVEALED

This isn't your first trip to the circus. Find out who you were the last time around.

In a past life, you managed to get married and divorced seven times. One spouse was semi-famous.

In a past life, you ran a speakeasy frequented by the mayor, the governor, and the local sheriff.

In a past life, you were bitten by six rats and died of the bubonic plague before age 17.

In a past life, you were a slave who hauled stones to build one of the Egyptian pyramids.

In a past life, you were a mad scientist who tried to make your own eyes shoot lasers.

In a past life, you had 19 children and put them all to work on your rural Kansas farm.

In a past life, you were wrongly accused of being a witch and locked in the stocks.

In a past life, you loved book burning, tent revivals, and rhubarb pie.

AM I NINJA MATERIAL?

All those rad moves look like fun, but let's find out if you'd really hack it.

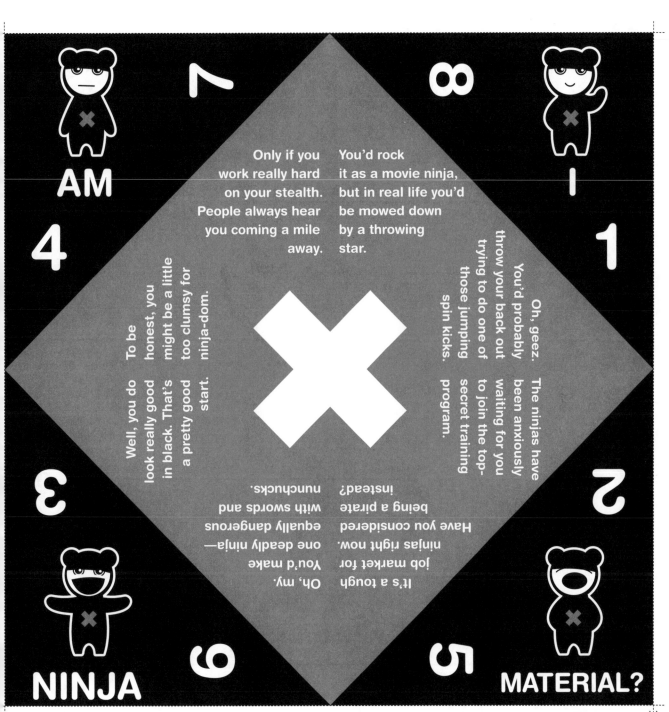

AM 7 8 4 1

Only if you work really hard on your stealth. People always hear you coming a mile away.

You'd rock it as a movie ninja, but in real life you'd be mowed down by a throwing star.

Oh, geez. The ninjas have been anxiously waiting for you to join the top-secret training program. You'd probably throw your back out trying to do one of those jumping spin kicks.

To be honest, you might be a little too clumsy for ninja-dom. Well, you do look really good in black. That's a pretty good start.

Oh, my. You'd make one deadly ninja—equally dangerous with swords and nunchucks.

It's a tough job market for ninjas right now. Have you considered being a pirate instead?

3 2 6 5

NINJA **MATERIAL?**

WHAT IS MY ARCHETYPE?

Even the best stories—movies, novels, comic books—rely on stock characters. Here's yours.

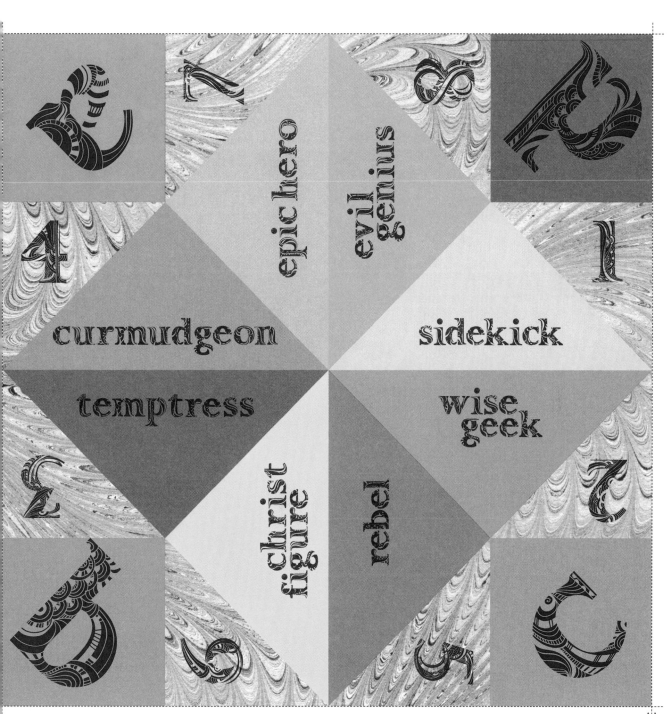

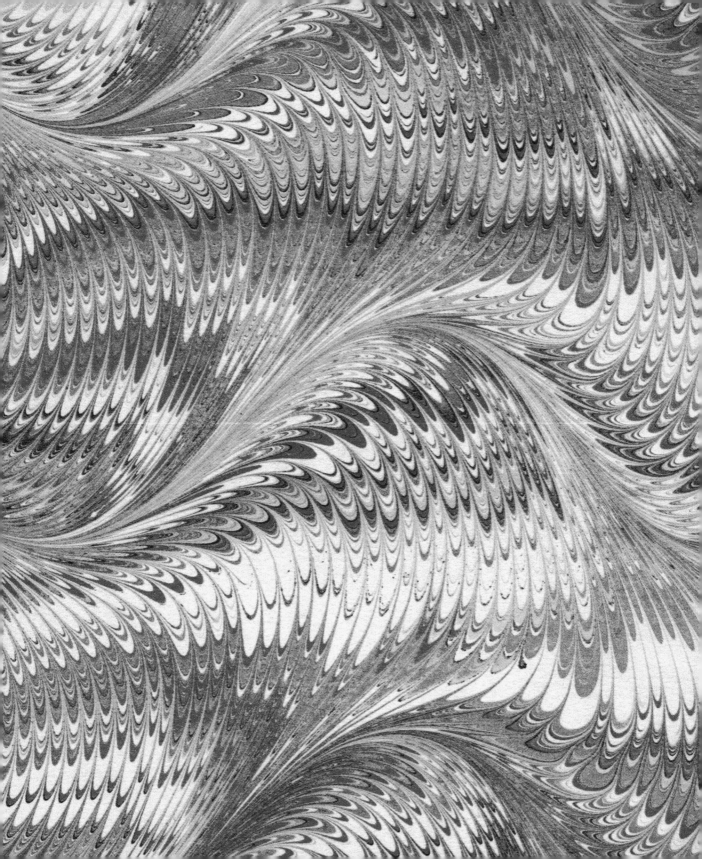

DOES THAT MEAN WHAT I REALLY THINK IT MEANS?

Song lyrics. Slang. Big words. Text message abbreviations. See if you're in the right.

slang

lingo

buzz word

jargon

7

8

4

1

3

2

9

5

6

You've stumped this cootie catcher. Better get a second opinion from the almighty Google.

Yes. But we don't expect you to fall into total cultural irrelevance for another 10 years.

Umm, no. It means something really X-rated that we're not going to repeat here.

No. You're pretty skewed on your understanding of this particular item.

We're not sure. But we recommend asking someone between the ages of 15 and 25.

Yes. Now take a moment to congratulate yourself for keeping up with the times.

Not even close. You're totally out of touch on this one.

Yep. It means just what you think it means.

FORTUNES FOR CUBICLE WORKERS

Those grayish-brownish dividers are starting to close in. Better find your work fortune now.

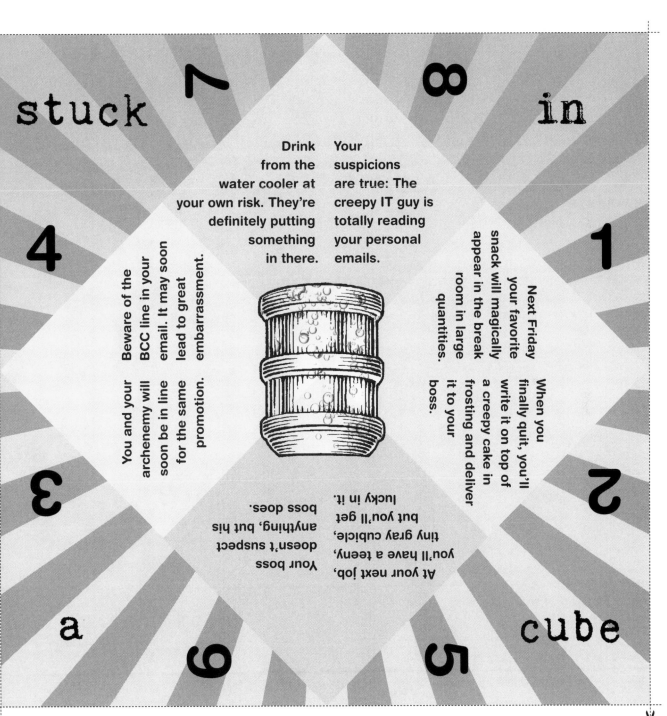

stuck 7

8 in

4

1

Drink from the water cooler at your own risk. They're definitely putting something in there.

Your suspicions are true: The creepy IT guy is totally reading your personal emails.

Beware of the BCC line in your email. It may soon lead to great embarrassment.

You and your archenemy will soon be in line for the same promotion.

Next Friday your favorite snack will magically appear in the break room in large quantities.

When you finally quit, you'll write it on top of a creepy cake in frosting and deliver it to your boss.

3

2

a

cube

6

5

Your boss doesn't suspect anything, but his boss does.

At your next job, you'll have a teeny, tiny gray cubicle, but you'll get lucky in it.

MAKE YOUR OWN: THE STYLE-OVER-SUBSTANCE VERSION

This one just looks really cool, OK? Fill in the fortunes however you see fit.

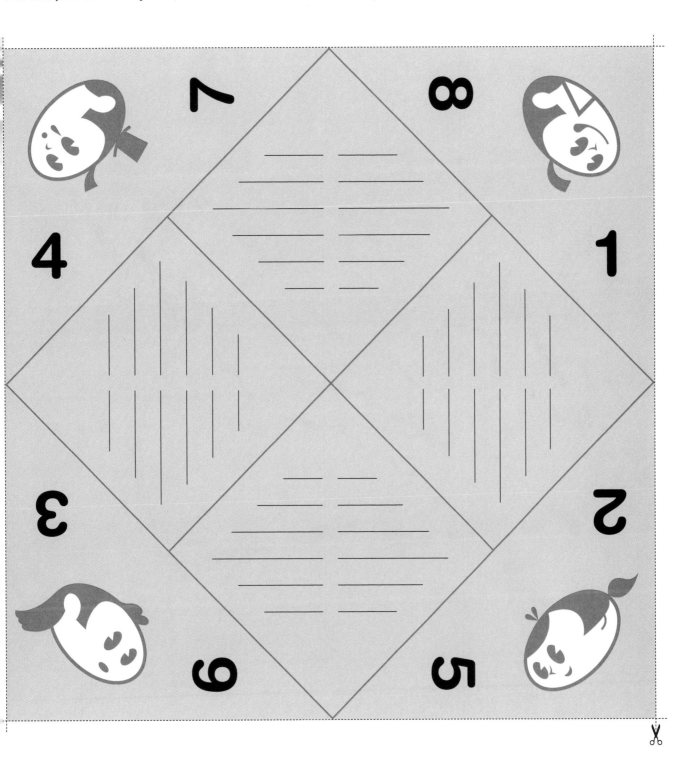

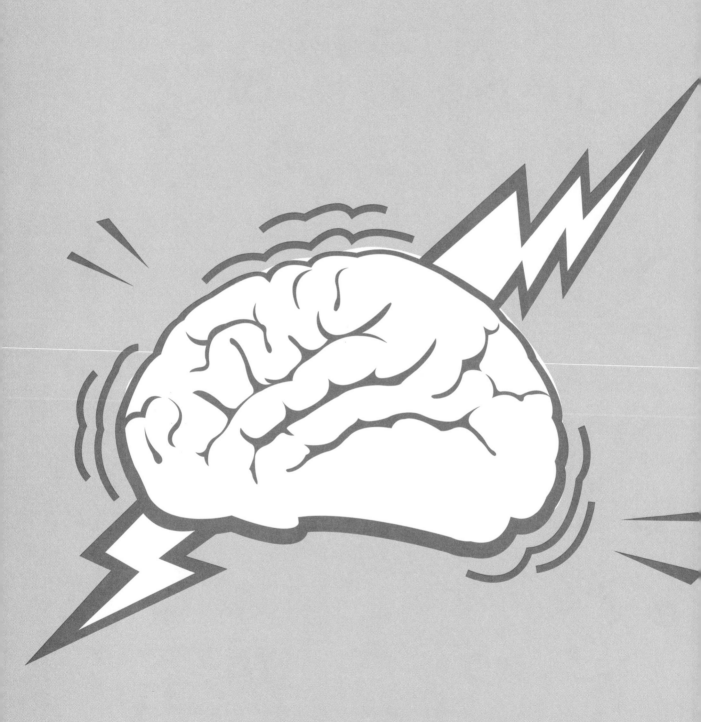

WILL I EVER SOLVE A RUBIK'S CUBE?

It's not your imagination. Those little colored squares are mocking you as you read this.

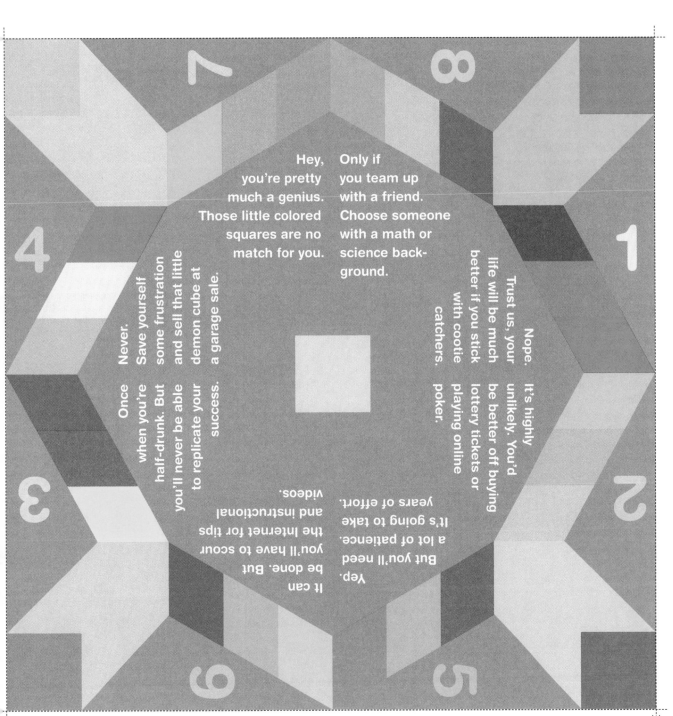

Hey, you're pretty much a genius. Those little colored squares are no match for you.

Only if you team up with a friend. Choose someone with a math or science background.

Nope. It's highly unlikely. You'd Trust us, your life will be much better off buying better if you stick lottery tickets or with cootie playing online catchers. poker.

Never. Save yourself some frustration and sell that little demon cube at a garage sale.

Once when you're half-drunk. But you'll never be able to replicate your success.

It can be done. But you'll have to scour the internet for tips and instructional videos.

Yep. But you'll need a lot of patience. It's going to take years of effort.

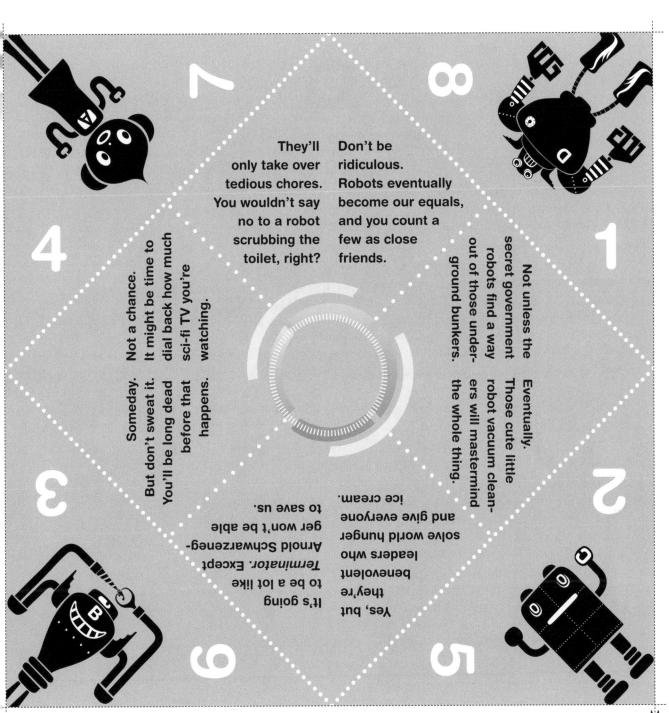

WILL ROBOTS TAKE OVER?

OK, robots might seem stupid, but they could be up to something. Something big.

They'll only take over tedious chores. You wouldn't say no to a robot scrubbing the toilet, right?

Don't be ridiculous. Robots eventually become our equals, and you count a few as close friends.

Not a chance. It might be time to dial back how much sci-fi TV you're watching.

Not unless the secret government robots find a way robot vacuum cleaners will mastermind out of those underground bunkers. Those cute little ground bunkers.

Eventually. the whole thing.

Someday. But don't sweat it. You'll be long dead before that happens.

It's going to be a lot like *Terminator*. Except Arnold Schwarzenegger won't be able to save us.

Yes, but they're benevolent leaders who solve world hunger and give everyone ice cream.

7 8 4 1 3 2 6 5

WILL I BE BROKE FOREVER?

The bank account looks pretty lean these days. Let's hope its future is brighter, er, greener.

1 **7** **8** **2**

4 **1**

You're going to become super obsessed with coupons, and it moves you into the middle class.

Probably. Unless you decide to start stealing copper plumbing from abandoned houses.

Not forever, exactly. But you may spend a decade looking for change under the couch cushions.

Yes. Unless you can find a creative way to start to move up several tax brackets. Spending Monopoly money. Nope. You're about Not entirely sure how.

Your luck is about to change. Are you up for a new job or a raise or something?

There's a windfall in your future: Expect an inheritance from a reclusive distant relative.

No way. You're going to build up a nest egg by working as a medical test subject.

3 **2**

3 **9** **5** **4**

FUNNY OR TOTALLY OFFENSIVE?

A joke. An online video. A comment. A photo. Run it by this foolproof litmus test.

7

8

4

1

Comedy gold. You should have your own TV show or Tumblr or something.

Rude. Crude. And if we could think of one more rhyming word, we'd throw that in, too.

Totally funny. (Unless you happen to be totally uptight.)

Hilarious. You just made this cootie catcher LOL. What? You didn't hear it?

Really, really offensive. Maybe even criminal. Keep this one to yourself.

It's so funny that if we had a nose, we'd be snorting milk out of it.

It's distasteful, insulting, and nauseating.

Good thing it isn't lunchtime.

Rethink your standards.

Even Howard Stern would find that reprehensible.

WHOOPEE CUSHION

3

9

5

2

SHOULD I GO VEGAN?

Illustrated by Jungyeon Roh

Let's face it. Your diet isn't anything to write home about. Find out if it's time for a big change.

HOW MANY KIDS WILL I HAVE?

Ah, parenthood. Crying babies. Dirty diapers. Surly teens. Let's see what the future holds.

Just one. It's a girl, and she's going to be pretty awesome.

No kids. But you'll have a wide variety of pets. Maybe even a giant lizard.

You'll have six kids, but your life will be nothing like *The Brady Bunch*.

Three. All boys. Really rowdy crazy boys who play every sport known to man.

You don't become a parent, but you do totally rock it out as an aunt or uncle.

Hmm. You'll either have two kids or 23—the psychic reading is fuzzy.

Two kids. Eventually, they'll both spend years in therapy.

There are multiples in your future. Twins, triplets, or maybe even sextuplets.

AM I (ACCIDENTALLY) DATING OUTSIDE MY POLITICAL PARTY?

Sometimes a donkey falls for an elephant. Without realizing right away.

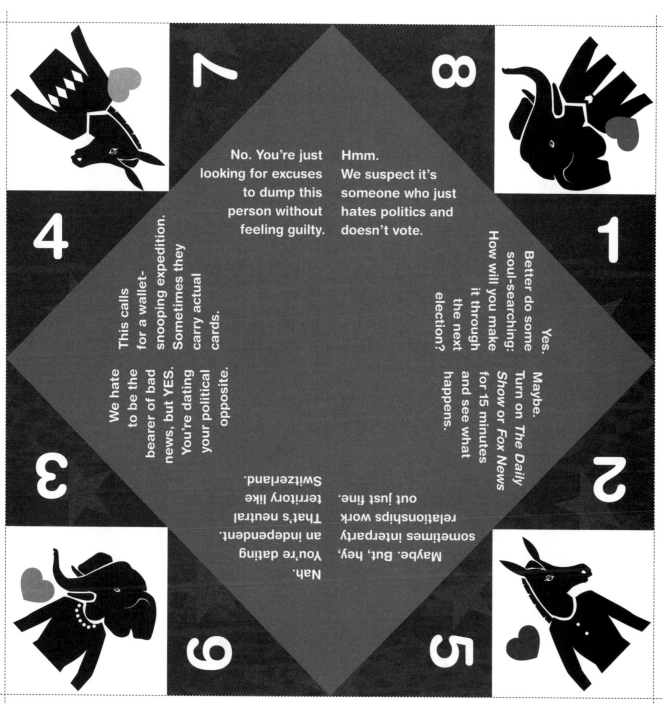

7 No. You're just looking for excuses to dump this person without feeling guilty.

8 Hmm. We suspect it's someone who just hates politics and doesn't vote.

4 This calls for a wallet-snooping expedition. Sometimes they carry actual cards.

1 Yes. Better do some soul-searching: How will you make it through the next election?

Maybe. Turn on *The Daily Show* or *Fox News* for 15 minutes and see what happens.

3 We hate to be the bearer of bad news, but YES. You're dating your political opposite.

6 Nah. You're dating an independent. That's neutral territory like Switzerland.

5 Maybe. But, hey, sometimes interparty relationships work out just fine.

WILL THIS CONFERENCE CALL EVER END?

This is serious. Someone could die from boredom if this phone meeting doesn't end soon.

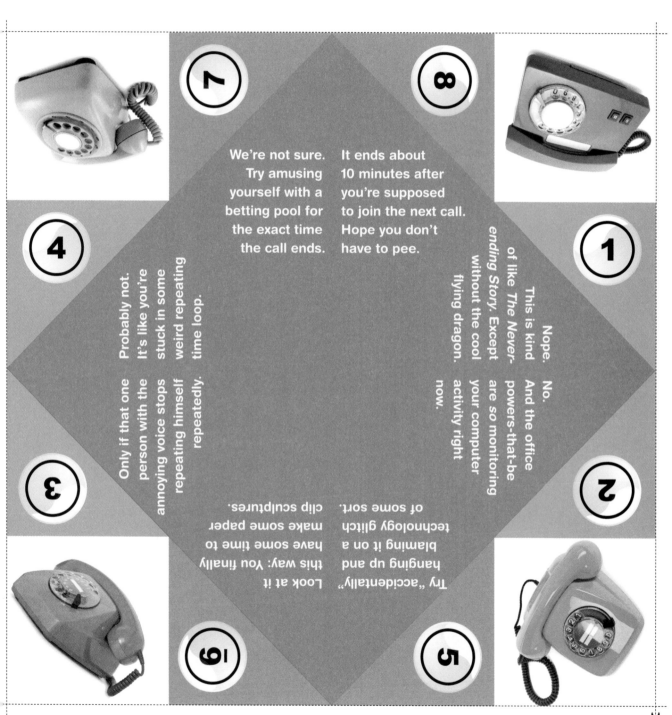

7. We're not sure. Try amusing yourself with a betting pool for the exact time the call ends.

8. It ends about 10 minutes after you're supposed to join the next call. Hope you don't have to pee.

1. Nope. No. This is kind of like *The Never-ending Story.* Except the office powers-that-be are so monitoring your computer without the cool flying dragon. activity right now.

4. Probably not. It's like you're stuck in some weird repeating time loop.

3. Only if that one person with the annoying voice stops repeating himself repeatedly.

6. Look at it this way: You finally have some time to make some paper clip sculptures.

5. Try "accidentally" hanging up and blaming it on a technology glitch of some sort.

EMERGENCY EXCUSE GENERATOR

Sometimes you just need to get out of something. Try these foolproof, on-demand excuses.

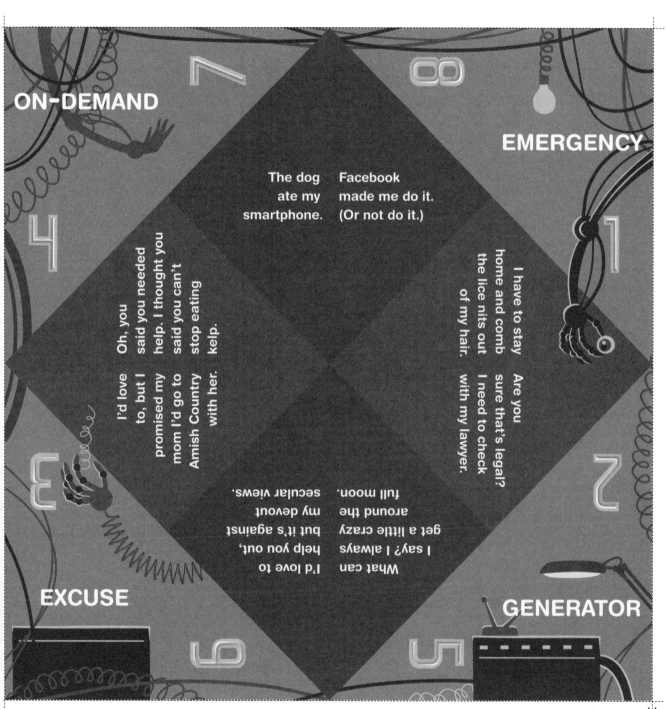

STILL SINGLE, STILL DATING

Don't despair. This cootie catcher looked into your romantic future. Advice and predictions within.

A

7

8

B

4

1

If back hair is a deal breaker, you'll never get married.

The person you're hoping will ask you out is going to send you three vague text messages next week.

Your next blind date will involve a bald man or a woman with a faint mustache.

Apparently, your soul mate is a homebody, so it might be challenging for the two of you to meet.

Your mom wants to fix you up on a blind date. Don't return her calls for at least a week.

Your next significant other will be fabulous in bed but hated by all your friends.

3

2

Your next date will rock, so don't wear that cartoon character underwear.

Sexting doesn't count as playing hard to get. Try a new tactic.

C

6

5

D

AM I A POSER?

Oh, sure, you look the part. But do you have the substance to back up the style and lip service?

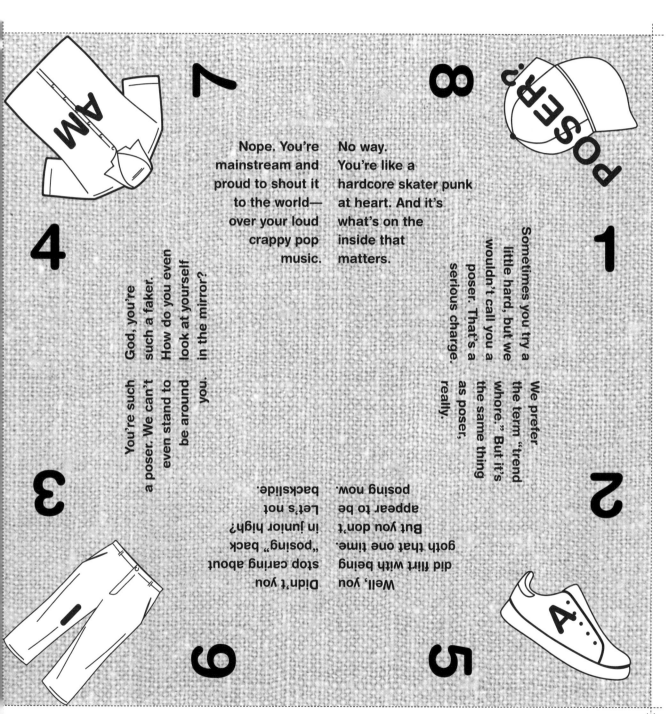

7

8

POSER?

AM

4

1

Nope. You're mainstream and proud to shout it to the world— over your loud crappy pop music.

No way. You're like a hardcore skater punk at heart. And it's what's on the inside that matters.

Sometimes you try a little hard, but we wouldn't call you a poser. That's a serious charge, really.

We prefer the term "trend whore." But it's the same thing as poser,

God, you're such a faker. How do you even look at yourself in the mirror?

You're such a poser. We can't even stand to be around you.

3

2

Didn't you stop caring about "posing" back in junior high?

Well, you did flirt with being goth that one time. But you don't appear to be posing now. Let's not backslide.

9

A

5

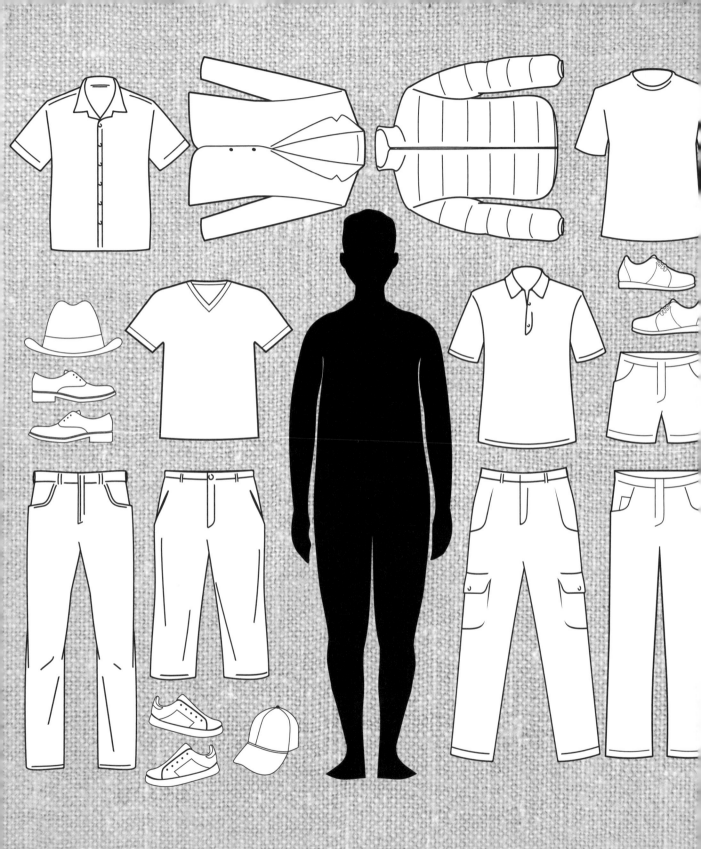

IS MY MOM RIGHT?

Oh, moms, always generous with the unsolicited advice. Double-check her latest wisdom.

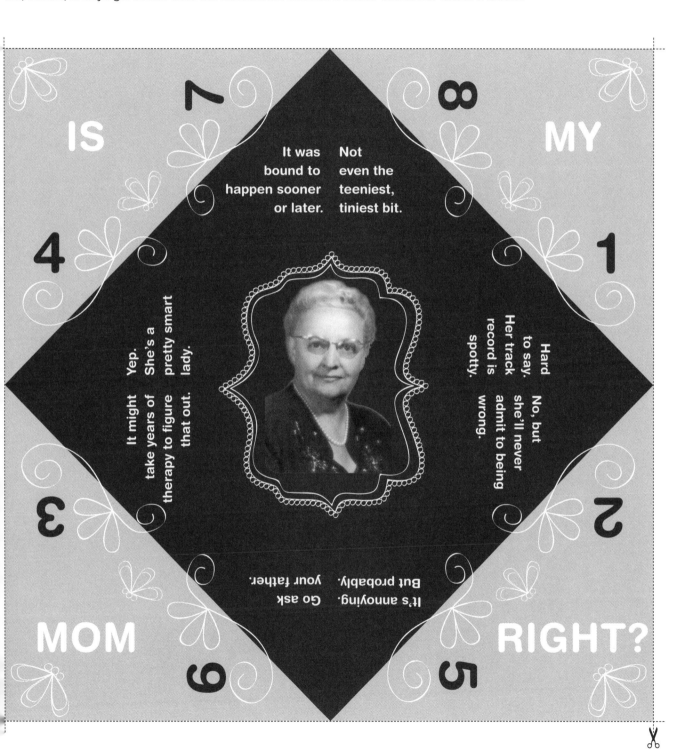

IS

MY

MOM

RIGHT?

7

8

4

1

3

2

9

5

It was bound to happen sooner or later.

Not even the teeniest, tiniest bit.

Yep. She's a pretty smart lady.

It might take years of therapy to figure that out.

Hard to say. Her track record is spotty.

No, but she'll never admit to being wrong.

Go ask your father.

It's annoying. But probably.

MAKE YOUR OWN: THE BLANK SLATE VERSION

No theme or prompts here. Let your imagination go wild as you fill in this cootie catcher.

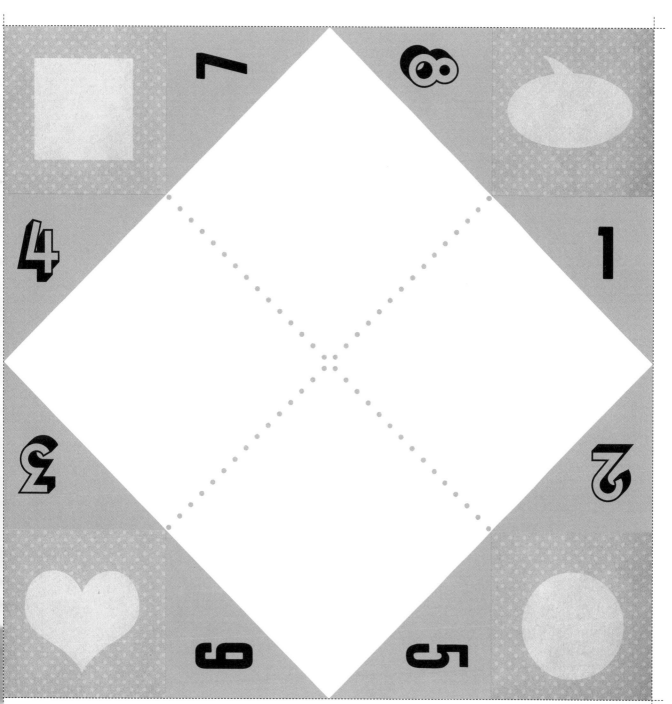

You're the creative type. Go ahead and make up another cootie catcher with custom fortunes.

COOTIE-FREE CONTRIBUTORS

(aka Super-Talented Guest Illustrators)

Stefan G. Bucher is the man behind 344design.com and the popular online drawing and storytelling experiment dailymonster.com. His books include *100 Days of Monsters, You Deserve a Medal: Honors on the Path to True Love*, and *344 Questions: The Creative Person's Do-It-Yourself Guide to Insight, Survival, and Artistic Fulfillment*. His time-lapse drawings appear on the Emmy Award–winning TV show *The Electric Company* on PBS and online as part of *A Show with Ze Frank*. He also created the titles for the motion pictures *The Fall, Immortals*, and *Mirror, Mirror* by director Tarsem.

San Francisco illustrator and fine artist **Lisa Congdon** (lisacongdon.com) was raised in both upstate New York and Northern California. Her vast catalog of paintings, drawings, collages, and repeat patterns is most often themed around her passion for nature, geometrics, and folk pattern. Lisa lives in the Mission District of San Francisco with her partner, her Chihuahua, and two cats. She works in her colorful studio a few blocks from her home.

Katy Fischer earned a BFA in design and printmaking from Drake University and has exhibited locally, nationally, and abroad. Her work is small, intimate, and speckled with relics of others' forgotten pasts. Currently, you can find Katy working as a creative director at TOKY Branding + Design in St. Louis. When she's not working, she's procrastinating.

Jessica Jones (jessicajonesdesign.com) is a graphic designer based in Evanston, Illinois, specializing in branding and identity, marketing collateral, and surface design. Along with logos, brochures, and print ads, her work includes a line of fabrics used on everything from purses to furniture. Her textiles have appeared on products at Nordstrom, Target, and the Land of Nod, and turned up in magazines such as *Glamour* and *Family Circle*. In her spare time, Jessica writes a popular design and DIY project blog called *How About Orange* (http://howaboutorange.blogspot.com).

A native Ohioan, **Ben Patrick** is a professional designer, illustrator, and animator. He has previously worked as a costumed mascot and an art gallery curator, and he had a brief stint with the circus, but his current day job is in advertising. By night, he can be found meandering around the interwebs, quietly rocking the guitar, pwning noobs online, and seeking out the worst movies. He lives in Cincinnati with his lovely first wife and an ever-expanding menagerie of small creatures.

Nicole Ray (nicoleray.com) is an artist and illustrator based in southeast Michigan. She graduated from the School of Visual Arts in New York and Trinity College in Connecticut. Nicole creates a line of whimsical art prints and paper goods infused with a playful sense of humor under the name Sloe Gin Fizz. Her daily rhythms are fueled by bottomless cups of coffee, towering stacks of books, and ginger-filled dreams of savory and sweet flavors. Nicole and her mister recently moved to a log cabin on a lake where they are happily cultivating a growing network of critter friends.

Originally from Seoul, Korea, **Jungyeon Roh** (jungyeonroh.com) is a New York–based award-winning illustrator who draws her Eastern and Western experiences primarily in silkscreen. The self-proclaimed full-time vegan and part-time pescetarian recently was named one of *Print* magazine's 2012 "20 under 30" new visual artists. She currently lives and works in Manhattan.

Brooklyn-based graphic designer **Ed Roth** founded Stencil1 (stencil1.com) in 2004. Many, including Martha Stewart, the *New York Times*, *ReadyMade*, and *Country Living*, have praised his iconic, reusable stencils. Stencil1 stencils can be used to paint walls, T-shirts, furniture—anything you want! Ed has done customized DIY events for clients such as Hugo Boss and the Gap. He also does large-scale stencil installation work for the Ace Hotel NY and Benjamin Moore, among others. His sixth release with Chronicle Books, *Stencil Style 101*, is available now.

Aimee Sicuro's whimsical vignettes invite us to see the world through her rose-colored glasses. Drawing inspiration from her own experiences and environment around her, Aimee (aimeesicuro.com) illustrates daily from her brownstone studio in Brooklyn, New York. She has clients in publishing and retail, and has exhibited work in San Francisco, Manhattan, and New Hampshire. Currently, she is working on a new series about relationships and the sometimes stumbling journey of women in their thirties.

Noah Scalin (alrdesign.com) is the creator of the Webby Award–winning art project Skull-A-Day. His fine art has been exhibited in museums and galleries internationally, including the Mütter Museum in Philadelphia and the International Museum of Surgical Science in Chicago. He is the founder of the socially conscious design firm Another Limited Rebellion, and he cofounded the Alternative Speakers Bureau. He has written five books: *The Creative Journey, Unstuck: 52 Ways to Get (and Keep) Your Creativity Flowing at Home, at Work & in Your Studio, 365: A Daily Creativity Journal, Skulls*, and *The Design Activist's Handbook*, coauthored by Michelle Taute.

THANKS A MILLION

A huge, huge thank-you to everyone who helped make this book possible. All the guest illustrators who enthusiastically gave their time and talents to this project. My editor, Meg Leder, for encouraging me to turn my daily creative project into a book. Noah Scalin for inspiring that daily creative project in the first place. Marla Beck for giving me the nudge to follow through with the idea. All my officemates at Cincinnati Coworks who answered 5,000 technical questions about my paper fortune-tellers blog (and cheered me on). Tricia Bateman for creating many early design elements. Kelly Kofron for turning my ideas and fortunes into tiny handheld works of art. Everyone else who took the time to visit paperfortuntellers.com, offer up awesome topic ideas and general encouragement, or otherwise show their cootie catcher love!

And last, but definitely not least, a heartfelt thank-you to my husband, Tom, for never ever asking why on earth I was spending so much time making cootie catchers (even when I was asking myself). Love you, Rio.

IMAGE CREDITS AND COPYRIGHT NOTICES

100% accurate answers to any yes or no question
Letters: Sasha Chebotarev/Shutterstock.com
Numbers: Katarina Fox/Shutterstock.com
Back pattern: Betacam SP/Shutterstock.com

Will I ever be rich or famous?
Numbers: readymade/Shutterstock.com
Pattern, art, and microphone: iStockphoto/
  Thinkstock

I'm breaking up with you (with this cootie catcher)
Front pattern: John T. Takai/Shutterstock
  .com
Back art: UltraViolet/Shutterstock.com

Will a shark attack?
Water: Marino Bocelli/Shutterstock.com
Sharks: tsaplia/Shutterstock.com
Feet/pool: Robert Crum/Shutterstock.com
Bandage: Chepko Danil Vitalevich/
  Shutterstock.com

Will I live with my parents forever?
Wood: 5AM Images/Shutterstock.com
Letters: iStockphoto/Thinkstock
Needlepoint: iofoto/Shutterstock.com
Frame/background (on back): caesart/
  Shutterstock.com

Will my credit card get declined?
All art: iStockphoto/Thinkstock

Am I a good kisser?
Lips: ariman/Shutterstock.com

Satin: Alexpi/Shutterstock.com
Kiss: jmcdermottillo/Shutterstock
  .com

Am I high maintenance?
Women: RetroClipArt/Shutterstock.com
Pattern: Icons Jewelry/Shutterstock.com

Emergency self-confidence booster
All art copyright © by Jessica Jones
  (jessicajonesdesign.com)

I forgot your birthday, but here's a cootie catcher
Girl/cake: Ivana Forgo/Shutterstock.com
Type: monbibi/Shutterstock.com
Pattern: Togataki/Shutterstock.com
Frame: blue67design/Shutterstock.com

Instant lie detector test
Graph paper: iStockphoto/Thinkstock
Letters: Hemera/Thinkstock
Fingers: Lisa S./Shutterstock.com

My '80s movie alter ego
Numbers: Yayayoyo/Shutterstock.com
Pattern: Kratueng/Shutterstock.com

I really, really hate you
People: ollyy/Shutterstock.com
Images used for illustrative purposes only
  and people depicted are models.

I really, really love you
All art copyright © by Lisa Congdon
  (lisacongdon.com)

Do I have bedbugs?
Bugs: MorphartCreation/Shutterstock.com
Mattress: Hemera/Thinkstock
Hand with vacuum: Dorling Kindersley RF/
    Thinkstock

Does my boss secretly hate me?
Numbers: yienkeat/Shutterstock.com
Stickies: Elnur/Shutterstock.com
Guy: Jupiterimages/BrandXPictures/
    Thinkstock

Make your own: Best friends forever
Letters: vecstock.com/Shutterstock.com
Papers: IntsVikmanis/Shutterstock.com
Doodles: notkoo/Shutterstock.com

Does my crush like me back?
Faces: yusuf doganay/Shutterstock.com
Pattern: Togataki/Shutterstock.com
Hearts: blue67design/Shutterstock.com

My Jane Austen character
Frames: sniegirova mariia/Shutterstock.com
Women: lynea/Shutterstock.com
Paper/script: iStockphoto/Thinkstock

Why is the sky blue?
Sky: LeksusTuss/Shutterstock.com
Planes: sntpzh/Shutterstock.com

Calorie-free emergency cupcakes
Cake: Aaron Amat/Shutterstock.com
Cupcakes: Ruth Black/Shutterstock.com
Frosting: Vlue/Shutterstock.com
Sprinkles: optimarc/Shutterstock.com

Am I in love?
Brain: Morphart Creation/Shutterstock.com
Heart/frame: vectorkat/Shutterstock.com
Pattern: DeMih/Shutterstock.com

Will my cat video go viral?
Fur: cla78/Shutterstock.com

Top left cat: George Doyle & Ciaran Griffin/
    Stockbyte/Thinkstock
Top right cat: Tony Campbell/Shutterstock
    .com
Bottom left cat: Hannamariah/Shutterstock
    .com
Bottom right cat: Ewa Studio/Shutterstock
    .com
Cats on back: S.P./Shutterstock.com

The imaginary animal advisory panel
All art copyright © by Nicole Ray (nicoleray
    .com)

Who is my celebrity love match?
Star doodles: iStockphoto/Thinkstock

**Make your own: The two-faced monster
version**
Monster: fongman/Shutterstock.com
Pattern: iStockphoto/Thinkstock

Real or fake?
Bag: Sam DCruz/Shutterstock.com
Wig: Hemera/Thinkstock
Boobs: Jeff Thrower/Shutterstock.com
Ring: Julia Reese/Shutterstock.com
Premium & authentic: iStockphoto/
    Thinkstock
Deluxe: oculo/Shutterstock.com
100% natural: Varijanta/Shutterstock.com
Pattern: iStockphoto/Thinkstock

Will I go to hell?
Pentagram: Hemera/Thinkstock
Sky: iStockphoto/Thinkstock
Sign: iStockphoto.com/tacojim

The Fortune Cookie Cootie Catcher
Green paper: FWStudio/Shutterstock.com
Pink paper: Hemera Technologies/AbleStock
    .com/Thinkstock
Animals: Patrickma/Shutterstock.com
Fortune cookies: Brooke Becker/Shutterstock
    .com

Will I die young?
Type: Hemera/Thinkstock
Illustrations: Igorij/Shutterstock.com

Friend or frenemy?
Numbers: natsa/Shutterstock.com
Illustration: Hemera/Thinkstock

Is it time to shave my beard?
Foam: pockygallery/Shutterstock.com
Beards (front side):Transfuchsian/
    Shutterstock.com
Beard (back side): Mike McDonald/
    Shutterstock.com
Pattern: ILonika/Shutterstock.com

Am I being followed?
Map: Hemera/Thinkstock

Make your own: The let's celebrate version
Dot diamond: sniegirova mariia/
    Shutterstock.com
Numbers: readymade/Shutterstock.com
All other art: iStockphoto/Thinkstock

What would Mr. T do?
Van and rings: Hemera/Thinkstock
Beard and hair: -Transfuchsian/
    Shutterstock.com
All other art: iStockphoto/Thinkstock

Will my novel/album sell?
All art: iStockphoto/Thinkstock

Where the f%&k is my soul mate?
All art: iStockphoto/Thinkstock

What kind of monster am I?
All art copyright © by Stefan G. Bucher
    (dailymonster.com)
Daily Monster is a registered trademark
    of Stefan G. Bucher. All rights
    reserved.

Make your own: The birthday card version
Paper and dot background: sniegirova
    mariia/Shutterstock.com
Candles and type: iStockphoto/Thinkstock

Which statement glasses are for me?
"A" guy: JamesWoodson/DigitalVision/
    Thinkstock
"B" and "D" girls: Jupiterimages/
    BrandXPictures/Thinkstock
"C" guy: JamesWoodson/Photodisc/
    Thinkstock
Glasses: Reno Martin/Shutterstock.com
Eye chart: My Portfolio/Shutterstock.com

I totally messed up. Please forgive me.
Type: readymade/Shutterstock.com
Center art and back pattern: Susanne
    Krogh-Hansen/Shutterstock.com
Stripes: Yuriy Boyko/Shutterstock.com

Am I a fashion victim?
All art: R_lion_O/Shutterstock.com

Important messages from cute puppies
Fur: luckypic/Shutterstock.com
Henry: WilleeCole/Shutterstock.com
Sophie, Ned, Zoey: Eric Isselee/Shutterstock
    .com
Puppies (on back): Gary Jones/Shutterstock
    .com

Marriage proposal by cootie catcher
Numbers: vintage vectors/Shutterstock.com
Illustration: Almog Ziv/Shutterstock.com

What would Cleopatra do?
Cleopatra: Andreas Meyer/Shutterstock
    .com
Letters: Hemera/Thinkstock
Snake ring: Hein Nouwens/library.com

So I'm turning 21
All images: iStockphoto/Thinkstock

My reality TV fate
All images: iStockphoto/Thinkstock

Would I make it as a graffiti artist?
All art copyright © by Stencil1 Inc. (stencil1
.com)
Design by Ed Roth of Stencil1

Is that vague Internet post about me?
Hands: NLshop/Shutterstock.com
Pattern: tovovan/Shutterstock.com

A talking Cyclops
Cyclops: Simonox/Shutterstock.com
Head and monster (on back): lineartestpilot/
Shutterstock.com

An instant psychic reading
Globe corners: Lana L/Shutterstock.com
Eye: Cyborgwitch/Shutterstock.com
Black and white photo: Everett Collection/
Shutterstock.com

Make your own: The sappy love note version
Letters: paulrommer/Shutterstock.com
Flowers: Anna Chelnokova/Shutterstock.com
Numbers: Kittisak/Shutterstock.com
Wood: donatas1205/Shutterstock.com

Is living alone making me peculiar?
All art copyright © by Aimee Sicuro
(aimeesicuro.com)

Fortunes for struggling rock musicians
All photos: iStockphoto/Thinkstock

Should I say hi?
Clouds: A-R-T/Shutterstock.com
Birds: Mrs. Opossum/Shutterstock.com
Paper texture: locote/Shutterstock.com
Bird pattern: artist_collion/Shutterstock.com

A pretty paper flower bouquet
Type: Lavandaart/Shutterstock.com

Flowers: Subbotina Anna/Shutterstock.com
Dots: donatas1205/Shutterstock.com

Am I a hoarder?
All images: MCarper/Shutterstock.com

Should I go swimming?
Swimmer photo: Everett Collection/
Shutterstock.com
Tricolor, green, and red beach balls: Le Do/
Shutterstock.com
Pink beach ball: Kesu/Shutterstock.com
Inflatable ring: J. Helgason/Shutterstock.com

Rock the baby shower
Corner pattern and letters: iStockphoto/
Thinkstock
Dot pattern: LeonART/Shutterstock.com

Make your own: Truth or dare?
Type: Callahan/Shutterstock.com
Numbers: natsa/Shutterstock.com
Illustrated guys and art on back: softRobot/
Shutterstock.com

Should I have another cocktail?
All art copyright © by Katy Fischer

Does Santa think I'm naughty or nice?
All art: iStockphoto/Thinkstock

**I'm quitting this job (with this cootie
catcher)**
Quit letters: AER/Shutterstock.com
All other art: iStockphoto/Thinkstock

Tattoos and me
Letters: Hemera/Thinkstock
Wire: PremiumVector/Shutterstock.com
Tattoo art: antipathique/Shutterstock.com

Fling or relationship material?
Pink panties, gray briefs and blue boxers:
iStockphoto/Thinkstock

Nude briefs: Hemera/Thinkstock
Cherry pattern: jane87/Shutterstock.com

Will I do jail time?
All art: iStockphoto/Thinkstock

How many donuts can I eat without throwing up?
1 donut: bernashafo/Shutterstock.com
2 donuts: spaxiax/Shutterstock.com
3 donuts, 4 donuts: Aaron Amat/Shutterstock
    .com
Box of donuts: mikeledray/Shutterstock.com
Paper: c12/Shutterstock.com
Pattern (on back): Shaun Newton Studio/
    Shutterstock.com

Make your own: A very scary Halloween
All art copyright © by Noah Scalin
    (noahscalin.com)

Feel better super soon
Type and numbers: readymade/Shutterstock
    .com
Soup: Pipko/Shutterstock.com
Light orange: Anna Sedneva/Shutterstock
    .com
Dark orange: topseller/Shutterstock.com
Flower: Luis CarlosTorres/Shutterstock.com
Smile plate: KKulikov/Shutterstock.com
Soup: Ilizia/Shutterstock.com
Tea cup: sniegirova mariia/Shutterstock
    .com
Tea mug: Petr Malyshev/Shutterstock.com

The hipster wedding decoration
Numbers and letters: williammpark/
    Shutterstock.com
Ornament: iStockphoto/Thinkstock
Frame, birds and ring: vecstock.com/
    Shutterstock.com
Swash (on back): Hemera/Thinkstock
Banner (on back): vecstock.com/Shutterstock
    .com

Did I overshare?
All art: iStockphoto/Thinkstock

I really, really miss you
Paper: Togataki/Shutterstock.com
Clouds and umbrella: Anna Paff/
    Shutterstock.com
Bunnies: svinka/Shutterstock.com

Would I survive a horror movie?
Background: Triff/Shutterstock.com
Letters: iStockphoto/Thinkstock
Doll parts: PHOTO FUN/Shutterstock.com
Dolls (on back): Hazeelin Hassan/
    Shutterstock.com

Important messages from my subconscious
All art: Limonov/Shutterstock.com

Am I a Cylon?
All art copyright © by Ben Patrick

Will anyone kiss me on New Year's Eve?
Letters: paulrommer/Shutterstock.com
Clock: Hemera/Thinkstock
Girl: Everett Collection/Shutterstock.com
Confetti: ANCH/Shutterstock.com

Will I get promoted?
Ladders and clouds: iStockphoto/Thinkstock
Sky: Comstock/Shutterstock.com

When will I get laid again?
Turtles and bugs: Hemera/Thinkstock
All other art: iStockphoto/Thinkstock

Is my drunk friend going to vomit in my car?
All images: sniegirova mariia/Shutterstock
    .com
Images used for illustrative purposes only
    and people depicted are models.

Is there a serial killer in the closet?
All images: iStockphoto/Thinkstock

My past life revealed
Diamond: Hemera/Thinkstock
All other art: iStockphoto/Thinkstock

Am I ninja material?
Ninjas: Trapeznikava Katsiaryna/
    Shutterstock.com

What is my archetype?
Marbled paper: iStockphoto/Thinkstock
Type: Stella Caraman/Shutterstock.com

Does that mean what I really think it means?
All art: iStockphoto/Thinkstock

Fortunes for cubicle workers
Water cooler: Jupiterimages/liquidlibrary/
    Thinkstock
Water: Hemera/Thinkstock

Make your own: The style-over-substance
version
All art: Oxley/Shutterstock.com

Will I ever solve a Rubik's Cube?
All art: Login/Shutterstock.com

Will robots take over?
Robots: Oxley/Shutterstock.com
Circle art: Hemera/Thinkstock

Will I be broke forever?
Pennies: iStockphoto/Thinkstock
Coin purse, girl: lynea/Shutterstock.com
Numbers: adinugroho89/Shutterstock.com
$1: Andrei Kuzmik/Shutterstock.com
$5: Quang Ho/Shutterstock.com

Funny or totally offensive?
Corner art: Dynamic Graphics, 2007/
    liquidlibrary/Thinkstock
Chevron: Togataki/Shutterstock.com
Flushing toilet: iStockphoto/Thinkstock

Should I go vegan?
All art copyright © by Jungyeon Roh
    (jungyeonroh.com)

How many kids will I have?
Numbers: natsa/Shutterstock.com
Bunnies: smilewithjul/Shutterstock.com
Orange background and carrots:
    iStockphoto/Thinkstock

Am I (accidentally) dating outside my
political party?
Flag texture: sunnyfrog/Shutterstock.com
Animal men: iStockphoto/Thinkstock

Will this conference call ever end?
Numbers: Hemera/Thinkstock
All other art: iStockphoto/Thinkstock

Emergency excuse generator
Numbers: McVectors/Shutterstock.com
All other art: iStockphoto/Thinkstock

Still single, still dating
Couple art: Laralova/Shutterstock.com
Love bomb: wongstock/Shutterstock.com

Am I a poser?
Cloth: Hemera/Thinkstock
All other art: iStockphoto/Thinkstock

Is my mom right?
Photo (on back): Stockbyte/Thinkstock
All other art: iStockphoto/Thinkstock

Make your own: The blank slate version
Numbers: vintage vectors/Shutterstock.com
All other art: sniegirova mariia/Shutterstock
    .com

Make your own: The then-again version
Numbers: Kittisak/Shutterstock.com
Cats: iStockphoto/Thinkstock

ABOUT THE AUTHOR

You might say **Michelle Taute** is a little obsessed with paper fortune-tellers. In 2011, while other people trained for marathons and wrote novels, she set out to make a cootie catcher every day for a year. She didn't quite make that goal, but she managed to create more than 300 paper fortune-tellers (and counting)—possibly more than any other thirtysomething in the world. You'll still find her posting and making new paper fortune-tellers on her blog at paperfortunetellers.com.

When she's not dreaming up cootie catcher fortunes, Michelle works as a writer and content strategist. She creates compelling copy for magazines, blogs, websites, scrappy entrepreneurs, and really big brands. Michelle's articles have appeared everywhere from *Better Homes and Gardens* and *Woman's Day* specials to *Metropolis*, *Communication Arts*, and *USA Weekend*. She's also the coauthor of *The Design Activist's Handbook* with Noah Scalin. Keep up with her latest projects at michelle taute.com.

ABOUT THE DESIGNER

Kelly N. Kofron's graphic design career has spanned almost 20 years. Specializing in print publication design, she worked as an award-winning art director for *I.D. Magazine* before starting her freelance business as provider of book and magazine design and production, magazine redesign, publishing consulting, and illustration. She has worked for such clients as Coffee House Press, Writer's Digest Books, Emmis Publications, St. Mary's Press, *Writer's Digest Magazine*, *HOW Magazine*, *Package Design*, *print*, *Horticulture*, *Hospitality Style*, and *VMSD*. She's also spent time as a board member and volunteer for AIGA/Cincinnati.

Kelly currently resides in Cincinnati with her super-smart husband, Matt; her two lovely children, Anna and Michael; and an old black Lab named Olivia. Find more about Kelly and her work at kofrondesign.com.